Faith Breaks, Volume 3
Even More Thoughts on Making It a Good Day

J. Howard Olds

WordStream Publishing, LLC
Nashville, Tennessee

Copyright ©2013 by the estate of J. Howard Olds

All rights reserved. Written permission must be secured from the publisher to use or reproduce any part of this book, except for brief quotations in critical reviews or articles.
For permissions and rights, email: **info@WordStreamPub.com**

ISBN-13: 9781935758136 (paperback)

Printed in the United States of America

1 2 3 4 5 6 7 8 9 10

Faith Breaks, Volume 3 is dedicated to
my three grandchildren, who are
immeasurable comfort and joy to me.
Caleb, Ella and Carrie,
remember Poppy loved you!
—Sandy Olds

Contents

Acknowledgements vii
Foreword ix

Attitude.. 1
Enriching Your Life 13
Have Faith 24
Family 35
Forgiveness 48
Identity and Values 58
Life Lessons 70
Peace 83
Perserverance 94
Relationship with God 106
Direction and Purpose 116
Sports 130
Storms in Life 140

Acknowledgements

My husband Howard Olds spent his life serving God by helping others. As a Methodist pastor for all of his adult life, he helped folks in every aspect of their daily lives. He was there through the countless births, baptisms, weddings, funerals, and all of the highs and lows in between. He had a gift with words and he has left behind a treasure of words. One might say that these words have served their purpose and could also be laid to rest. However, as the keeper of the treasure of these words, I have felt that their messages were still relevant and needed in today's world.

Faith Breaks, through the years, have become known—mostly to radio audiences in Kentucky and Tennessee—for their messages of hope and help. One of Howard's favorite songs was "If I Can Help Somebody." The lyrics go like this:

> If I can help somebody
> As I travel on
> If I can cheer somebody with a word or song
> If I can keep somebody
> From travelin' wrong
> Then my livin' shall not be in vain.

Publishing Faith Breaks in book form has been possible only with generous support and help of some very special people. Dr. Jack Fletcher and friends at Brentwood United Methodist Church in Nahsville, Tennessee helped to make the first volume a reality. My friend, Jan Knight, wrote prayers and sorted and organized scripts for *Faith Breaks,* Volume Two. Volume Three has required a host of helpers, and I could never have accomplished this without the encouragement and time-consuming contributions of several church friends.

First I want to thank Emily Hewgley for offering her nimble fingers on the keyboard and her quick mind in sorting through hundreds of pages of text. Gary Dowdy offered to help me one day as we ran into each other in the grocery, having no idea what he was getting himself into! Gary had published devotions in *The Upper Room* so he was a natural in writing the poignant prayers at the end of each script. Three couples shared the task of reading the scripts and making appropriate revisions or editorial suggestions. They are Tom and Rosemary Blose,

Ed and Cheryl Minnich, and Jim and Gail Perkins. I am especially grateful to Ed for scanning and converting the outdated type into a usable format. Linda Young volunteered months ago to proofread for me if I ever needed her help. I am so thankful for her keen attention to detail and for polishing the completed document.

Thank you all so much! You saw this as "God's work," and I pray that God will be glorified by our combined efforts.

I continue to be grateful for publisher Roger Waynick, who had the vision for these books but sadly did not live to see the finished product. And, I am grateful to Marti Williams of WordStream Publishing who worked to see Roger's vision become reality. Marti has demonstrated that these little devotionals still have something valuable to communicate, now five years after Howard's death. Thank you, Marti.

Finally, thank *you*, Reader, for taking time for a Faith Break.

— *Sandy Olds, 2013*

Foreword

After retiring from the Episcopacy in 1996, my wife and I started worshipping at Brentwood United Methodist Church in Brentwood, Tennessee. Dr. Howard Olds became Senior Pastor of the church in 2000. We would listen to Howard proclaim the faith from the pulpit on Sunday morning, and we would give attention to the Faith Breaks he shared during the week on a local radio station. Dr. Olds offered Faith Breaks to morning commuters for decades. These were short inspirational messages aimed at helping the listener to make every day a good day. His inspired messages were heard by the congregation on Sunday and by people on the streets of life during the week. This book contains many of those messages.

Those who read *Faith Breaks* will discover that Dr. Olds was a modern day Barnabas. Barnabas, according to the book of Acts, means "son of encouragement." Faith Breaks have an infectious way of giving encouragement to those who are seeking to live life to the fullest. They encourage us to be kinder, friendlier, more loving, and less critical people. Good, solid advice is given about not sitting on our dreams and the importance of letting our souls catch up with our bodies.

Faith Breaks calls upon us not to have our hands so full of ourselves that we cannot notice the good that is in other people. Howard Olds would want us to look for the good that is in all people. *Faith Breaks* helps us to do just that.

Theologically, Dr. Olds is calling us to show our love for God by loving other people. His writing draws us nearer to God so that we can be brought nearer to the needs of others.

Howard Olds wrote and shared his Faith Breaks but he never broke faith with the highest calling of the Christian faith. I have been inspired and helped by these inspirational writings. My hope is that you will also be encouraged by this modern-day Barnabas.

— *UMC Bishop Joe E. Pennel, Jr., 2013*

Attitude

Crabs

Fishermen say you never need a top for a crab basket. If one crab starts to climb up the sides of the basket, the other crabs will reach up and pull it back down. There are people who act a lot like crabs.

In a competitive world, it is easier to weep with those who weep than it is to rejoice with those who rejoice. We can sympathize with failure better than we can congratulate success. We are jealous of those who rise too high and succeed too quickly. We want to pull them back in the bucket where they belong.

What if we replaced the spirit of competition with the spirit of cooperation? What if people helped each other climb as high as they can without yielding to the temptation to cut them down? What if service became our motto instead of selfishness? What kind of world would we have?

So the next time you see someone doing well, cheer them on instead of holding them back. After all, people were not made to live like crabs.

Put within us wise God, the need to give encouragement to others rather than the desire to "tear them down." Help us to be better than crabs. Amen

Affirmation

"Don't tell him that he's good, it might go to this head"—I've heard that all my life and now I wonder why are we such jealous guardians of another's humility? Affirmation does not produce pride. Affirmation increases assurance, confirms self esteem, and encourages self worth. Most people's heads are not puffed up with self importance, but infected with self doubt and fear of failure. The internal critical parent is forever questioning every accomplishment, eroding every joy. We add to it when we keep honest praise from another for fear it might go to his head.

Why not try a better way? The praise and encouragement of significant others is critical in establishing a positive self image and producing productive people. So let's rejoice in each other's joys, embrace our children's happiness, and enhance a friend's future by honestly saying, "You did a good job, and I am proud of you!" It can make all the difference.

Oh God – help us to learn affirmation.
Help us to give praise and encouragement to our children,
support our fellow workers, and rejoice in the
happiness of others. Amen.

Atmosphere

An astronaut was asked by a reporter to name the key to successful space travel. Without batting an eye the astronaut replied, "The secret to traveling in space is to take your own atmosphere with you." I've found that true for travels on earth, too. How about you?

The air in some rooms is filled with negative criticism. Breathe enough of it into your soul, and you will become critical too. Fill a meeting with talk of despair, and pretty soon the most positive people feel the doom of gloom. As my wise English teacher used to say, "Some people are just born in the objective case." Whatever the subject, they are against it. Given such attitude pollution, people are wise to take their own atmosphere with them. Such people provide a breath of hope in a room of despair, a positive note in a climate of criticism, a reason to move on against the objections of the day.

The next time you feel the affects of attitude pollution, do what the astronauts do—take your own atmosphere with you.

Joyful God, fill me with your joy and goodness so I can share with others an atmosphere of optimism. Let me be the one to change the mood in the room. Amen.

Bumper Stickers

People make a habit of expressing themselves on bumper stickers these days. If you want to know what a person is for or against, believes deeply or supports strongly, just follow them a few blocks and read the one liners on their bumpers.

Driving downtown recently, I read these two contrasting messages on the bumpers of motorists. One said, "Good Happens," and the other read, "Born Against." Both vehicles were driven by adult men. I began to wonder what was going on inside each of them.

A school teacher mentor of mine used to say, "Some people are just born in the objective case." I suppose that was true of the man in the Mustang. Whatever the nature of the day, the substance of proposals, the suggestions of others, his vote was already in. He was born against it.

On the other hand, the man in the pick up truck believed good to be possible, surprises to be positive, the days to be hopeful. He believed that good happens.

It all got me thinking. What kind of message do I leave on the streets of life, if not on my bumper, certainly through my contacts with people throughout the day?

Our Father in Heaven, what message am I leaving behind in my life? How would my bumper sticker read? Would others see that I am a Christian by my actions? Lead me to be the person you would have me be! Amen.

Blowing Horns

A car stalled at a green light. It stopped and wouldn't start. The cars behind kept honking their horns out of frustration that the car was blocking traffic. Finally, the driver of the stalled car walked back to the honking motorists, pecked on the window, and said, "My car is stalled and won't start. If you would like to try to start it for me, I'll be glad to sit here and blow your horn."

The old saying is true. Before we criticize or abuse, honk our horns, or blow a fuse, it is always wise to walk a mile in the other man's shoes. From a distance, we can never understand why people won't work, and why others won't choose to do as we do. From a distance, it's easy to be critical of those who fail their children and miss the mark of their high calling. All along the fact remains; we do not live in their skins nor deal with their circumstances. Caring people seek first to understand. In the meantime, they refrain from tooting their own horns.

We are quick to judge others!
Gracious Lord, teach me to have
patience and understanding.
Encourage me not to blow my horn,
but offer assistance. Amen.

Helpfulness

I was standing on a street corner in Manhattan recently, trying to read a street map when a banker on his way home from work stopped to help. In a brief moment, he gave me precise and clear directions to my desired destination, and in one random act of kindness, he changed my opinion about New Yorkers. While visiting the city, we saw wonderful plays, examined normal tourist sites and experienced outstanding music. But my lasting impression of New York City was made by people on the street corners and subways who were willing to help me find my desired destination. "Has New York changed, or have my assumptions of the city always been wrong?"

It would probably do us a world of good to re-examine a lot of our preconceived notions about people and places. Most people can be trusted. The majority of people want to be helpful. Most strangers are not predators. So why do we let the actions of a few form our opinions of the whole? Yes, we need to be wise and alert, but let us not surrender to mistrust and fear.

Thank you God for those who reach out to others and offer help in times of need. Helping others is so easy. Why do we make it so hard? Inspire us gracious Lord to answer this call! Amen.

Whistling

When our four-year-old grandson paid us a visit a few weeks ago, he couldn't wait to show us that he had learned to whistle. In fact, he was so proud of himself that he couldn't seem to stop whistling. He whistled while he played. He whistled while he walked. He whistled in the car. He whistled everywhere.

As I shared my grandson's new found joy, I began to realize that I do not whistle as often as I used to. Life has done something to my song. The sorrows of life have robbed me of the joys of life so much that I have lost my habit of whistling.

When children rejoice they laugh and play, dance and sing, and yes, even whistle. They let their joys be known. And, they invite others to join them.

So, how about it? Are you whistling a tune as you travel along? Are you cheering somebody with a word or a song? Is your positive attitude keeping others from traveling wrong? If so, your living will not be in vain.

Loving God, help me to be more like the child who whistles, sings and laughs. Remind me to remember the joys of life. It's contagious! Amen.

Trust

"You just can't trust anyone anymore!" Do you embrace that belief?

Steven Brill decided to challenge that theory in New York City. Brill went undercover as a well-to-do foreigner with little knowledge of English. He got into several dozen taxi cabs to see how many drivers would cheat him. What do you think happened? Only one driver out of thirty-seven did him in. The rest took him directly to his destination and charged him correctly. Several refused to take him when his destination was only a block away. Some even got out of their cabs to give him directions. Most warned him to be careful as New York City was full of crooks.

Trust is an ultimate value that protects civilized society from chaos. Maybe people are more honest, trustworthy, respectable and responsible than we think. At least I hope so. And as for me, I can determine to be so.

Dear Lord, you are a trusting God.
You love us no matter what we do.
Help us to trust others as you trust us.
Put within our hearts your goodness
and love so that we will also
earn the trust of others. Amen.

Newcomer

A newcomer to our city asked the clerk at the Post Office the nature of people living here. The wise postal worker asked, "What sort of people lived in the city you left?" The newcomer replied, "Oh, people back there were grumpy, selfish, rude, and dishonest."

"Then you'll probably find people here to be about the same," said the postal employee.

Hours later, another newcomer to our city asked the same clerk the same question? "What kinds of people live here?"

Once more the wise postal worker inquired, "What sort of people lived in the city you left?"

"Oh, people back there were kind, generous, friendly, and anxious to help," said the newcomer.

"Then you'll probably find people here to be about the same," concluded the clerk.

In every community, birds of a feather tend to flock together, and people are likely to attract others of similar mind and attitude. So, if we want a kinder, friendlier city we can start by being kinder, friendlier people.

Dear Jesus, show us how to live more like you.
Fill our hearts with the desire to be "kinder, friendlier"
people so that we will reflect your love to others. Amen.

Dreams

Larry Walters was a thirty-three year old truck driver who spent a lot of time in his back yard sitting in an old lawn chair wishing he could fly. Time, money, education, and opportunity, however, never allowed Larry to become a pilot.

Then one day, Larry took that old lawn chair and hooked forty-five helium filled surplus weather balloons to it. He tied a six pack of beer to one leg, peanut butter and jelly sandwiches to the other leg. He strapped a parachute on his back, a C.B. radio to his big trucker belt, and laid a B.B. gun across his lap to pop the balloons when he wanted to come down.

Larry thought he would go up about two hundred feet. Instead, he soared eleven thousand feet which got him the attention of the Los Angeles International Airport and every news station in town. When Larry finally shot out enough balloons to return to earth, a reporter asked Larry. Why did you do such a thing? A smiling Larry said, "Sometimes you just can't sit there."

How about it, are you sitting on your dreams, or letting them lift you higher than you've ever been lifted before?

You know we have our dreams Lord.
You also know that many times we fail to act on them
due to our fear of failing. Give us the courage to follow our dreams
so that we can make the best of the life you have given us. Amen.

Vanity

Portraying Satan in the movie "Devil's Advocate," actor Al Pacino affirms vanity to be Satan's favorite vice and the 20th century his most successful season. The powerful movie examines one man's moral weakness in the face of outrageous material gain.

Well, how do you deal with vanity? To be vain is to be hollow, conceited, and proud. The vain sell their souls to the company store and compromise their families on the altar of success. To be vain is to win at all cost, prosper at any price, and succeed in every circumstance. Vain persons chase the wind, ignore the sin, and wind up paying more than they ever bargain for.

Vanity: resist it. Defy it. Never let it do you in. Overcome vanity with integrity, honesty, and a balance to life that brings out your best.

Dear Lord, help us to realize the danger of pride and self-centeredness. Place in us the strength to resist vanity by putting you first, others second, and ourselves last. Amen.

All Wound Up

A music box featuring a clown was displayed in a gift shop with this sign under it: "Clown is defective when wound up too tight."

Some anonymous shopper penciled in these words at the bottom of the sign: "Aren't we all?"

We live in an uptight world. This is the age of the half-read page, the bright night with the nerves tight, the plane hop with the brief stop, the lamp tan in a short span, the brain strain and the heart pain. The cat naps till the spring snaps, and the fun's done.

Because tension takes its toll on mind, body, and soul, healthy people learn how to unwind, slow down, relax, and rest. They know how to be still and be restored. They know how to let their souls catch up with their bodies. So if you are feeling the pressure of life, maybe its time to stop and worship the Giver of Life. It could make a world of difference! You see all clowns are defective when wound up too tight.

Dear God, we know that your word tells us in Philippians 4:7 that you offer us "peace that passeth all understanding." Help us to be ever mindful of this when we start to feel like our springs are getting too tight. Amen.

Enriching Your Life

Scarcity

In a *Family Circus* cartoon, Joey charges to the front of the line to get a piece of his own birthday cake. His mother, reminding him of his manners, asks Joey to let his guests go first. "But if they go first, I won't get the biggest piece," insists Joey as he charges straight ahead.

When it comes to the things of life, do you live by a mentality of scarcity or abundance? Is it your core conviction that there is only so much to go around, and you have to scrap for everything you can and protect whatever you have at all costs? Or, do you live in an attitude of abundance, assuming there is always enough for everybody? If you have an idea, share it. If you have money, give it away. There is more where that came from. If you have one piece of pie, let someone else have it. You can always bake another one. What would it be like to live that way?

Thomas Jefferson put it this way: "A candle loses nothing when it lights another candle." Love is something that always multiplies when you take the time to give it away.

Teach us to pass love on so that it is multiplied by others. It is not enough to live for ourselves. Show us how to share our love for others. In the name of our Loving Savior, Amen.

Time of Your Life

Having the time of your life! What would that mean to you? Would it be frolic and fun, a dream come true, some future hope that you got to do? Would it be freedom to do your own thing, chart your own course, and determine your own destiny? Having the time of your life, what would that mean to you?

In one sense, the time of our life is all we have, nothing more, nothing less, nothing else. We have the time of our lives. Such time can be used or abused, invested or wasted, fretted over or lived out, but you *know* this minute is the time of your life. Why not take this tiny sliver of a moment and determine to do something good with it?

The author of Ecclesiastes says there is a season to everything and a time for every purpose under heaven. Breathe deeply, walk gently, relate genuinely, and live fully, for this time of your life is a precious gift.

Dear Jesus, let this time of my life
be a precious moment to be lived fully and wonderfully! Amen.

Random Acts of Kindness

As I went to pay for my lunch the other day at a local restaurant, I discovered that some unknown person had already paid my bill. I was the recipient of a "random act of kindness." Since I do not know my benefactor, I cannot reciprocate. I am indebted to some unknown person of the universe. They even left a couple dollars in change with a message for me to enjoy some coffee in the afternoon.

While I can afford to pay for my own lunch, the random act of kindness brightened my day. It was an affirmation that good people still inhabit the earth. It was a subtle message that I still had worth. It was an unexpected joy in the middle of the routine that gave me hope for the rest of the way.

Are you spreading random acts of kindness? One thoughtful person traveling a toll road paid the fare for five cars behind them. A teenager scrubbed graffiti from a bench on campus. A shut-in writes five notes a day to friends, acquaintances, and strangers. We have the power to brighten the corner where we are. Why not start today?

Loving God, we have learned that when we help others through random acts of kindness that we are the benefactors. In so doing, we feel your love and we give you thanks for that! Amen.

Promises

Human relationships are held together by the silver thread of promises made and promises kept. Have you considered that?

A promise is like an island of certainty in a sea of the unknown. When a woman makes a promise, she reaches out into the unpredictable future and makes one thing predictable. She will be there even when being there costs her more than she wants to pay. When a man makes a promise, he stretches himself out into the circumstances that no one can control and controls one thing. He will be there no matter what the circumstances may be.

Are you a promise maker and a promise keeper? If you have a ship that you will not desert, if you have a people you will not forsake, if you have a cause you will not abandon, then you are one of those people who provide stability to a shaky world. If you are reliable and dependable, if you say what you mean and mean what you say, if you can be counted on no matter what, then keep on keeping on! The world is depending on you.

O Lord, give me the strength and courage to do what I say I will do, keep my promises, and show others that I am a person upon whom they can depend. In your Holy name I pray, Amen.

Yellow Ribbon

"Tie a Yellow Ribbon Round the Old Oak Tree" is a ballad about a man who has spent his time in prison giving the one who once loved him every right to reject him. Nevertheless, he writes her a letter saying he'll be passing by on a bus any day now. If she can find it in her heart to forgive him, he had one request: Would she tie a yellow ribbon round the old oak tree, so he would know whether to stop or pass on by?

The tension on the bus was incredible as it neared the bend where the woman lived. The parolee could hardly stand it. Then, to his surprise, his eyes beheld it. There were a hundred yellow ribbons tied to the old oak tree. Passengers cheered as the man found his way home.

Though we find ourselves estranged from God and significant others, we can go home again. Just like a lost sheep, God welcomes us back and says, "I love you my child, come on in!

Isn't it about time you turned your heart toward home?

It is comforting to know that you are the Good Sheppard and will welcome us back when we have strayed and lost our way. We give our thanks to you Loving God. Amen.

Simple Truths

Visitors at Annapolis noticed several students on their hands and knees assessing the courtyard with pencils and clipboards in hand.

"What are they doing?" inquired a visitor.

"Answering a question," replied the guide.

"Every year the seniors ask the freshmen how many bricks it took to finish paving the courtyard."

"And how many did it take?" continued the visitor.

Walking out of the student's hearing distance the guide answered, "One."

Are you ever tempted to make matters seem more complicated than they really are? Life does have its riddles. There are questions for which there are no easy answers, but life is not always as complex as we sometimes try to make it. God is good. Love never fails. Service supersedes self. Life lasts forever. We can debate such assertions. We can question them, analyze them, restate them, or try to explain them. Let not our inquiry rob us of peace and joy.

Simple truths are foundations on which to build a soulful life. Belief, hope, and faith are trustworthy avenues to life.

God of all, we give thanks for having faith
and knowing that love is the cornerstone of our lives.
Amen and Amen.

Gratitude

More and more, the singular word that describes my approach to life is the word "gratitude." I am grateful for the gift of life. I am grateful for a host of friends. I am grateful for my family. I am grateful for my freedom. I am grateful.

One of the special blessings of my present life is that of grandparenting. Grandchildren put us in touch with a simple wonder and joy that is easily forgotten in the complexities of making a living and meeting the demands of the day. When our five year old grandson visits, he always insists on saying the blessing for our meals. While he has several selections in his repertoire of prayers, he most often bursts forth singing these words: "0 the Lord's been good to me, and so I thank the Lord, for giving me the things I need, the sun, the rain, and the apple seed. The Lord's been good to me."

Whether or not we are aware of it, the Lord's been good to all of us. God has helped us carry every burden. Our every sorrow, God has shared. Whether our days have been sunny or dreary, God has been there beside us to hold us and guide us.

Wonderful God, we give thanks for life, friends, freedom, and for some of us, grandchildren. Most of all, we give thanks for your love that sustains us in all we do. Amen.

Middle Age

It has been said, "At twenty, you want to be the master of your fate and the captain of your soul." At fifty, you're inclined to settle for being the master of your weight and the captain of your bowling team. Middle age is when your glasses and your waistline get thicker, while your hair and your wallet grow thinner. In middle age, you don't give much thought to exercise and entirely too much thought to dinner.

Middle age is something that happens to us if we are fortunate enough to live that long. While it is definitely a passage in life, it need not be a crisis. Middle age is an opportunity to find our true selves and our spiritual bearings. It challenges us to refocus our lives according to priorities that stand the test of time. While it can be frightening to lift up the floorboards of our lives and examine the foundations, it need not lead us to foolish actions or crazy decisions. Fear not the maturing process; it could make you a better person.

Blessed Creator, life has many stages. Help me to enjoy all of them and make the most of each day. Whatever my age, let me rejoice, and guide me on my faith journey. Amen

Seeing

"Rhythma-Rhythma-Rhythma-ree. I see something you don't see." I found myself playing that childhood game with my grandson the other day. It saved him from boredom, until I could get him home and helped pass the time by absorbing the scenery. Since then, I've been thinking; calling attention to the overlooked sights all around us is a valid, attitude-altering experience for us all.

As Elizabeth Barrett Browning put it:

> "Earth is crammed with heaven
> And every bush is alive with God
> But only those who see take off their shoes
> The rest sit around and pick blackberries."

On a normal drive to work, there is a sunrise signaling the gift of a brand new day. There's an older brother assisting a younger sister across the street. There's a squirrel at play. Two lovers parting for work kiss good-bye. A neighbor stops by to say, "Hi." Oh, the sights and sounds of a normal day. Do you have eyes to see and ears to hear the wonders of life around you?

God, the opportunity to be thankful for the wonders of life is with us each day! Guide us to be observant so that we will see the beauty of your blessings that are before us. Amen.

Courage

Andrew Jackson once said, "One man with courage makes a majority." The world needs us to be people of courage. Courage is the strength to stand up when it's easier to fall down. Courage is the desire to maintain our integrity when it would be easier to look the other way. Courage is the determination to move forward when it would be easier to feel sorry for ourselves and quit. Courage is not the absence of fear, but rather the judgment that something else is more important than fear. Or, as I like to say, courage is fear that has said its prayers.

Are you a courageous person? Do you march to the beat of inner convictions or simply get in step with the crowd? Are you willing to ask the hard questions and take the heat of criticism? Take a stand, and dare to join the chorus of those who say, "Here I stand, I can do no other." One person with courage makes a majority.

Dear Heavenly Parent, help us to be courageous in the face of criticism and doubt. May all our fears become prayers! Amen.

Time

Carl Sandburg once said, "Time is the coin of your life. It is the only coin you have. Be careful, lest you let other people spend it for you."

So, how are you spending the time of your life? Time management experts tell us the average American in a lifetime spends 5 years waiting in line and six months waiting at traffic lights. We also spend one year searching for misplaced objects, six years eating, eight months opening junk mail, and two years trying to return telephone calls.

By contrast, the average married couple spends four minutes a day in meaningful conversation with each other and thirty seconds a day in dialogue with their children.

The days of our lives are 24 hours, 1,440 minutes, 86,400 seconds. Nothing more, and nothing less. Time is a precious divine gift. The use of time is a sacred responsibility. How we spend what we've got-well: that's what life is made of.

Dear God of eternity, help us to use your gift of time faithfully. May we use our time to love others, involve ourselves with meaningful interactions with people, and walk humbly with you. Amen.

Have Faith

The Bible

In a *Family Circus* cartoon, Dolly is reading her own version of the Bible. "Jesus helpers were the twelve opossums," announces Dolly. "Moses got the ten commandments at the top of Mount Cyanide. One of the commandments is 'Humor your mother and father.' Another one says, 'Thou shalt not admit adultery.'"

Over the years, I've noticed a lot of people have their own version of the Bible. With a Bible in hand, prejudices have been supported, people have been judged, children have been abused, and change has been avoided. With a Bible in hand, good news has become bad news and love has given way to hate. With a Bible in hand, Churches have split, people have lost jobs, and families have been torn apart.

I've also noticed that many people who quote the Bible have never really read it. Its themes of love and grace, justice and mercy have never been fully explored. Perhaps, if we are going to use the Bible, we owe it to ourselves and others to find a diverse group of people to help us interpret it. That's what some churches try to provide.

Dear God, you have given me the Bible
so that I might know of your love and be guided on my faith journey.
Help me to grow in my discernment by joining with others in my
church family to study your word. Amen.

Spirituality

Film maker George Lucas says, "I put the 'force' in the Star Wars Movies in order to awaken a certain kind of spirituality in young people. I wanted them to begin asking questions about mystery." It appears Mr. Lucas succeeded. In fact, the most extraordinary thing about the 20th century was the failure of God to die as many predicted, and a few announced.

The Beatles announced in the 1960's they were more popular than Jesus Christ. But, time took its toll on the Beatles. About thirty-five years ago, a philosophy professor at a prestigious university noted that God was dead. Now it seems the news of God's demise was greatly exaggerated. In fact, God seems to be doing quite well here at the end of a millennium. Professional wrestler turned politician, Jesse Ventura, announced recently that, "organized religion is a crutch for weak minded people." We'll see how long the governor's grandiosity endures.

Dear Lord, there are people in our world who want to deny your existence and remove you from our lives. You have been with us all the days of our lives including our yesterdays, our todays, and our tomorrows. Give us the strength to be witnesses to your existence by helping us to live Christian lives. Amen.

Worry

A woman, for years, had trouble sleeping at night for fear of burglars. Sure enough, one night she and her husband heard a noise downstairs. The husband went down to investigate. Low and behold, he discovered a burglar standing in their living room. The husband didn't panic. Instead, he walked up to the intruder and said, "Good evening, sir. I'm pleased to see you. I want you to come upstairs and meet my wife. She's been waiting to meet you for ten years."

Does fear fill you life and worry rob you of sleep? Do you exist in the constant anxiety that something bad is about to happen to you and your loved ones? While it's wise to be alert, it's wearisome to worry for worry soaks the joy right out of us.

So, let us live our lives by faith, not fear. No one knows what tomorrow holds or what trouble may lie around the corner. But, is any of that changed by worry? People of faith are confident that they have the courage to overcome whatever comes at them, so they live their lives with hope and joy.

Dear Lord, you told us not to worry about our tomorrows and that worry will not influence future events. Help us to live our lives by faith and with the knowledge that joy and hope will replace fear and worry. Amen.

Fear

Did you hear the story about a mother who was trying to tuck her toddler in bed on a stormy night? The mom was about to turn the light off when the kid said, "Mommy, will you sleep with me tonight?"

The mother smiled and gave the child a long hug and then said, "You know I can't sleep with you, I have to sleep with Daddy."

A very long silence was broken by a shaky little voice that said, "Daddy is a big sissy, isn't he?"

When it comes to the storms of life, what frightens you? While fear can be a friend of reindeer, rabbits, and humans—alerting us to danger ahead—things can also scare us, shock us, stun us in such ways that we are paralyzed from positive action. While a life without fear may be impossible, courage in the face of fear is essential. After all, about 60% of our fears are unfounded, about 20% are already behind us, and about 10% are too petty to matter. Of the remaining 10%, there's only about 5% that we can do anything about. So, maybe it's time to put our fears in perspective.

The storms of life pound us Lord so that we fear life's unknowns. Through prayer and faith we can overcome our fears and find strength from you to weather our storms. We ask that you continue to be with us and help us to keep our fears in perspective. Amen.

Resources

Remember that Fed Ex commercial in which an employee went down on a plane in a deserted island, managed to survive for five years, and finally delivered the package to a suburban home?

The bedraggled employee inquired of the customer, "May I ask what's in your package?"

"Oh nothing really," said the lady, "just a satellite telephone, a global positioning device, a compass, a water purifier, and some seeds."

What if the resources we need to survive in this world are closer than we think? God is only a prayer away. Friends care more than we imagine. Communities are capable of pulling together for good causes. Even strangers like to turn a good deed.

We have not been deserted. We are not alone. We live in God's world, and people are created with the capacity to care. So, look all around you; find the resources you need to meet the demands of the day. Use what you've got. Bloom where you are planted. Serve where you are needed. Help where you can. It could make all the difference.

We thank you, God, for the blessings we enjoy and for the resources you have given us. You have always provided for our needs and for that we offer our appreciation. Amen.

I Can

On the first day of school, a creative teacher had her 4th grade class write all their "I can'ts" on a piece of paper. You might imagine what they wrote:

"I can't kick a soccer ball."

"I can't do math very well."

"I can't make friends very easily."

"I can't get Debbie to like me."

When everyone had finished their assignment, the students in solemn procession placed their "I can'ts" in a decorated shoe box and marched outside to bury the thing.

"Friends," said the teacher, "we gather here today to honor the memory of 'I can't.' While he was on earth, he touched the lives of everyone. His name has been spoken in schools, city halls, state capitols, and yes, even the White House. May 'I can't' rest in peace, and may everyone present pick up their lives and move forward believing, 'I can.'"

All of us could use a teacher, a supervisor, a friend like that. What we need is not smaller mountains but greater climbing ability. What we need is not smaller challenges but greater confidence. Thank God for those—including some teachers—who believed in us long before we could believe in ourselves. To them we owe our praise, our thanks, and our deepest devotion.

Thank you dear Lord for putting people in our lives that can encourage and inspire us. This builds our confidence so that we can be all we can be. Amen.

Keep Sailing

Somebody said, "All the water in the world can't sink a ship unless it gets inside."

Try to remember that the next time you navigate through some stormy days of life. Storms do come. Winds blow. Floods rise. It is not unusual to find ourselves in deep water. In times like these it's the strength of the ship, not the intensity of the storm, that determines our survival.

A friend of mine bought a new boat. It had all the latest equipment: deep wells, fish finders, stereo, comfortable seats—the works. He was so anxious to get it in the water that he forgot to insert the plug. Imagine his embarrassment as the boat dropped off the ramp and filled with water.

Do you have a boat that will float in all kinds of weather? Will your ship keep you secure throughout eternity? Have you the faith, the determination, the stamina, the security to keep sailing regardless of the circumstances? Remember, all the water in the world can't sink a ship unless it gets inside.

Loving God, give us the faith, strength, and courage to navigate the storms of life. You are our captain and we ask you to also be the rudder for us and guide us through life's stormy seas. Amen.

Relatives

When Tammy Harris from Roanoke, Virginia, turned twenty-one, she began searching for her biological mother. After a year, she had not succeeded. What she didn't know was that her mother, Joyce Schultz, had been trying to locate her for twenty years. And, what neither Tammy nor Joyce realized, according to the Associated Press, was that they both worked in the same convenience store.

One day, Joyce overhead Tammy talking with another co-worker about trying to find her mother. Soon they were comparing birth certificates. Sure enough, mother and daughter had been in the same building working side by side. "It was the best day of my life," exclaimed Tammy as she held on to her mother for the longest time.

There is a deep longing in all of us to find our way home and be embraced by our Creator. The truth is that our heavenly Parent is closer than we think and nearer than we realize. Why don't you reach out and join the family, the family of God.

Loving God, what a joy it is to be a part of the family of God. Help those dear Lord who seek you to find their way home. Amen.

"Give a Hoot"

Did you hear about the apathetic owl that became so calloused with life that he just didn't give a hoot anymore? People can get like that too. Time and circumstances can leave us uncaring, unconcerned, unexcited, unmoved, and untouched. We get so discouraged that we just don't give a hoot any more. We feel like quitting.

If such feelings describe you, maybe it's time to consult a higher power. God likes life; God invented it. It is to the full, flowing, free life that God calls us. We are made to live, not merely survive. We are made to soar, not merely soak up the sun. We are made to put in more than we take out and live each day with eager anticipation.

So don't throw in the towel, blend into the woodwork, and forget your purpose for being. Keep moving forward, keep growing, and keep learning. It can make all the difference.

Creator of life, restore in us the joy of living.
We want to fully partake in life's blessings through
the love of your son, Jesus Christ! Amen..

Faith

Faith! You can't leave home without it. We live by faith not because we want to but because we have to.

Let me give you an example. We go to a doctor whose name we cannot pronounce, who writes us a prescription we cannot read, which we take to a pharmacist whom we do not know. He gives us a chemical compound that we do not understand and tells us to take the pill a few times a day in the sure and certain hope that it will make us feel better. If that is not faith, then what is?

If it takes faith to live our daily lives, then why is faith in God so hard for some of us? Perhaps God has disappointed us or let us down at some critical moment of life. We asked for help and God remained silent. Or, perhaps we've simply gotten used to doing our own thing and do not even think about a relationship with God.

Faith is the ability to believe it before we can prove it and the confidence to act before we have all the facts. Would you dare to take a leap of faith toward God today?

Help me dear Lord to grow in my faith and in my relationship with you. Let me dare to take a bigger leap of faith toward you today than ever before. Amen.

Life

Somebody said, "the problem with life is that it is just one darn thing after another."

Sometimes "darn" is not a strong enough word to describe it. Life does have its difficulties. Like a roller coaster, it has a way of lifting you up, slamming you down, and jerking you around, one curve after another, only to drop you off at the very spot you boarded in the first place.

But you know, in spite of all its difficulties, I like life. I like its joys and possibilities, its thrills and its chills, its challenges and its opportunities. Life can never be boring if you take the time to smell the roses or observe the beauty of one fall day. Life can never feel hopeless, if you face your fears with faith.

So I plan to live. I plan to live each moment and love each moment that I have on earth. And when my time comes, I plan to soar into worlds unknown with the sure and certain hope that I will live forever. You see, my days of living will not be past while life and breath and being lasts, or immortality endures.

So why not live instead of survive?

Maker of creation, you have blessed us with life's abundances. May we slow down the pace of our lives and enjoy the blessings you have given to us. Help us to live each moment as if it is our last. For we ask these things in Jesus' name. Amen.

Family

Realism

When Harry Truman was engaged to Bess Wallace he sent her this letter. "Since I can't rescue you from any monster or carry you from a burning building or save you from a sinking ship simply because I would be afraid of the monsters, couldn't carry you, and can't swim, I'll have to go to work and make money enough to pay my debts, and then get you to take me for what I am: just a common everyday man whose instincts are to be ornery, but who is anxious to be right."

With that proposal, Bess Wallace became Mrs. Harry S. Truman.

It is my observation that most engaged couples could add a dose of realism to their relationship. There is no person on earth who is going to meet all your imagined needs. Relationships are not forged on some fantasy island, but in the daily flow of work and responsibility. If couples became more realistic in their expectations, they might be more satisfied with their experiences.

O Lord, sometimes we are afraid to be honest with one another. Help us, trusting Father, to develop this trait when interacting with others. Inspire us to love each other as we are. Amen.

Marriage

"After sixteen years of marriage, with two kids and two careers in the making, my husband announced he was not happy in this marriage," writes Roberta Bondi.

What could have been an end for Richard and Roberta, turned out to be a growth point for both. Here's how they did it:

"1: We truly wanted to get through this conflict and not walk away from it.

2: We deliberately decided not to lie to each other nor make any effort to conceal the truth.

3: We each took responsibility for our own wrongs.

4: By accepting God's grace for our own shortcomings, we were equipped to ease up and listen to each other."

Marriages that last for a lifetime involve people who are able to turn a time of crisis into an opportunity for creative growth. They involve determined, dedicated people who know they are not perfect and do not demand perfection from others. In such a climate of mutual respect, change is possible. So the next time your relationship runs into a roadblock, don't cancel the trip. Rise instead to a higher road.

Show us how to be a good partner in marriage through loving, forgiving, and understanding each other. These traits come from you dear Lord. Teach them to us. Amen.

Successful Marriage

According to a poll by *USA Today*, the three most important factors in a successful marriage are mutual respect and trust, open regular communication, and marital fidelity.

The golden rule of treating others as you would like to be treated is a fundamental principle of healthy relationships. Marriage is not two people competing with each other for power and control. Marriage is two people joining hands to accomplish great things together. Mutual respect provides the framework for positive communication. People communicate effectively by speaking the truth in love and listening twice as much as they talk. Healthy communicators discover that vital balance of talking and listening. Former President Bill Clinton said he wrote the book *My Life* to encourage people to talk more openly about their mistakes. Had he really wanted to help the American family, he might have considered encouraging people not to follow his example of extra-marital affairs.

Marriage is a fundamental institution of human society. It deserves our respect, our attention, and our deepest devotion.

Creator God, you created man and women and gave us marriage as the foundation of community. Teach us to live together as man and wife based on love, mutual respect, and fidelity. Help us care for each other as ourselves. Amen.

Anniversary

My wife and I celebrated our 40th wedding anniversary recently. My how time flies and love matures through the years!

When love is young, it seeks to get. We like our significant other for what they can do for us. "He makes me happy." "She meets my needs." On such need-meeting terms, we are first attracted to others.

When love grows up, it seeks to share. Marriage is give and take and often a lot of compromise. Couples learn to bend without breaking and give without being consumed by the needs of the other. Marriage and family are shared responsibilities. When love matures it often includes sacrifice. Illness strikes. Children rebel. Trouble comes. When we walk through the valley of some unexpected trouble we are asked to give and keep on giving without receiving much in return. Here, love reaches its deepest level, the level of self-surrender.

It takes commitment, patience, and endurance for love to mature. That is why so many couples bail out before they become one. They give up before they get it together. No, marriage is not an easy road. It is however, worth the sacrifice.

O Lord, in our wedding vows we say these words, "for better or for worse." Yet, when times in our marriage become difficult we want to give up. You have taught us to seek patience and endure hardships so that love may mature and grow. Help us to remember our vows and your teachings. In Christ's Holy name we pray. Amen.

Keep Love Alive

"Successful marriage is a matter of two people meeting each others needs," says author Willard Harley.

According to Mr. Harley, the five top needs of a woman are these: affection, conversation, honesty, financial security, and family commitment. The five top needs of a man are: sexual fulfillment, recreational companionship, attractive spouse, domestic support, and admiration. How are you doing in the need meeting department of your marriage?

While no one can be all things to all people—and it takes more than a relationship to make any person happy—marriages that last are made up of people who try hard to meet each other's needs. Love goes the second mile and often gives more than is expected. Love that never ends tends to believe all things, endure all things, and hope all things. With lively imagination and enduring dedication couples can keep love alive through the years.

*Help us, O Lord, to keep love alive in our marriage.
We know that lasting love endures all things, believes all things, and
hopes all things. In the name of the Father,
Son, and the Holy Spirit. Amen.*

Forgetting

"When I argue with my wife she gets historical," complained a husband to a friend.

"You mean she gets hysterical?" asked the friend.

"No," replied the husband, "I mean historical. When we argue, she reminds me of every time I have failed her in the past."

If we are going to live at peace with our partners in this life, most of us will have to do some forgetting as well as forgiving. To forget is to let the past be past. To forget is to choose not to remember. To forget is to surrender your right to hold a grudge or nurse a wound.

Two friends were discussing the shortcomings of their husbands. "Don't you remember that time Joe let you down?" said one friend to another.

"No," replied the friend. "I distinctly remember forgetting that."

Such acts of the will can lead us to the restoration of emotion. How are you doing at this business of forgetfulness?

Dear Jesus, you have told us to forgive one another.
Help us learn that in the act of forgiving we must learn to forget
as well. Teach us how to forgive and forget the acts of others.
We ask it in your Holy name. Amen.

Just Like You

"Cat's in the Cradle" is a sobering song by the late Harry Chapin. It particularly causes fathers to stop and think.

> "My child arrived just the other day
> He came to the world in the usual way--
> But there were planes to catch and bills to pay
> He learned to walk while I was away.
> And he was talkin' fore I knew it.
> As he grew, he'd say
> 'I'm gonna be like you Dad,
> You know I'm gonna be like you someday.'"

The lyrics progress until the boy is grown and the father's retired. Dad phones his son, trying to get together sometime. But the boy's job's a hassle, the kids have the flu. There's little time to talk it through. The boy has grown up just like his dad. "They'll get together sometime," he said.

In trying to do the things that matter, let's remember the little ones that matter. They'll grow up to be like us, yes. They'll be just like us!

Merciful Parent, don't let me be like the father in this song. Help me to remember the little things that matter in life and be there when my children need me. Amen

Mothers

If your job demands 24 hours a day, 365 days a year; if you have no holidays, no vacation, no union, no automatic promotion, and no pay raises; if you received no training for your task, but are expected to be an expert teacher, counselor, administrator, nurse, taxi driver, chef and janitor; if the most frequent question asked you begins with "Hey, where's my..."—then you must be a mom. If not, then you are certainly a stay-at-home dad.

So as Mother's Day approaches, I say, "Hats off to Moms: the employed ones and the stay-at-home ones."

What happens at your house is more important than what happens at the White House. You are the real secretaries of defense and the keepers of the peace. In the routines of managing a house and making a living, you are shaping society for generations to come. You are a combination of pastor, physician, teacher, and counselor. It's no wonder you feel torn. Even so, the world is counting on you to hang in there. So keep on keeping on.

Dear Lord, thank you for mothers and their devotion. Bless them and give them the strength to love and nurture their families. In Jesus' name we pray. Amen.

Something Different

Thanks to modern technology, our homes are forever talking to us. Computers watch our children, tell us how to cook, and remind us when we forget to lock the doors. Thanks to the internet, we can instantly communicate with friends and strangers around the world.

While homes now talk to us through technology, I wonder, "Do we talk with each other in person?" Studies suggest interaction between parents and children average less than thirty seconds a day. Communication is the number one problem between couples. A revolution of people communication is needed alongside the conveniences of technology.

Why not do something different tonight? Turn off the TV, get off the Internet, turn on the telephone answering machine, and talk with one another for a change. Ask for what you need, and actively listen to the needs of others. Turn up the compliments as well as the complaints. Let your loved ones know they are loved and appreciated. The results could be revolutionary.

We are constantly using technology to communicate with one another. Wise God, slow us down and show us how to talk and listen to one another. We pray this simple prayer asking for your presence in this age of technology. Amen.

Touch

"Staying in touch." Now there's a saying with far reaching effects on health and wholeness.

Studies reveal that massaged babies are more active, alert, and responsive then untouched babies. They gain weight faster and are better able to calm and console themselves. Touched babies tend to have fewer physical problems.

What's true for infants holds true for all ages. We even express it in our language. Separated people tend to loose touch. We refer to a crisis in terms of "touch and go." When we are deeply moved by music, art, or religion, we describe the experience as touching.

Long after our eyes fail us, sounds elude us, mobility becomes impossible, and speech is no longer an option—even then, we can reach out and touch the people we love and find healing for our souls. So let's stay in touch with one another. It might make us all feel better!

*Good Shepherd, lead us in life to care for one another.
Let us remember that a simple touch or pat on the back shows
others that we care. Teach us dear Lord to be caring people. Amen.*

Please Come Home

As a young widow, Christiana did everything possible, working as a maid, to make a living for her daughter Maria. For fifteen years it seemed to be enough, but Maria, a beautiful girl, began to itch for a better life and one night slipped from her bed and caught a bus to the nearby city. Christiana knew Maria had no money and no way of survival. So she set out to find her. She stopped at a nearby drug store and took small pictures of herself. In the nearby city, she posted those pictures on every hotel bulletin board, barroom mirror, and telephone booth possible. Exhausted and broke Christiana returned home to wait. Weeks passed.

Then one morning, as Maria was descending the stairs of a cheap hotel, she saw a familiar picture on the bulletin board. It was the picture of her mother. On the back were written these words, "Whatever you have done, whatever you have become, I love you. Please come home." Maria Did.

God is like a caring mother, searching diligently for her children to come home.

Lord Jesus, you have told us that each person is precious in your sight. You have also told us that wherever we are or whatever we have done, you will take us back home to you. We give thanks for your unending love. Amen.

Children

A group of people gathered in a private home for a dinner party. Among the invited guests was a pastor. As folks took their seats at the table, the pastor was asked to give the blessing. He turned to the talkative six year old girl seated beside him and asked if she would take his place.

"I wouldn't know what to say," replied the suddenly shy young lady.

"Just say what you hear your mom say," encouraged the pastor.

With that the little girl folded her hands, bowed her head, and with a distressed voice said, "Dear Lord, why on earth did I invite all these people to dinner?"

Well, more than any parent wants to admit, our children do repeat the things we say and copy the habits we embrace. When our children duplicate our expressions, our words, our attitudes, or actions, it can be embarrassing to say the least. Example is life's greatest teacher. Blessed are those who have good role models in deed as well as word.

Dear Lord, as the old saying says, "The best sermon is preached before the talking starts." Put in our hearts the desire to live our lives as Christian role models for our children. Amen.

Fathers

"When I was a boy of fourteen," wrote Mark Twain, "my father was so ignorant I could hardly stand to have the old man around. But when I got to be twenty-one, I was astonished at how much he had learned in seven years."

I suspect most of us can identify with Mr. Twain.

Wisdom is something we come to appreciate over time. While not all fathers are wise, many possess the knowledge of experience that can save us from many a foolish notion. Fathers want the best for their children. They may not express it vividly nor emote it lividly, but way down in the depths of their hearts, they care. They really care. Wise fathers possess the patience to wait for their wisdom to be wanted instead of entering verbal battles with their offspring who are certain that old men don't know a thing. So this Father's Day take another look at the man you call "Dad." He may become smarter with the passing of time.

*Gracious God, you have taught us to honor our fathers.
Help me each day to show the love and respect for my father
that leaves no doubt in his mind that I love and honor him.
If I am blessed with children, guide me to be an example of
a Godly parent and a positive influence in their lives. Amen.*

Forgiveness

To Forgive

A *Primetime* special on ABC examined the story of a high school cheerleader who was brutally raped and murdered by three teenagers, two of whom she had dated. As the bizarre events unfolded, the pattern of drinking, drugs, and teenage naïveté became evident. Parents mourn. A community is shocked. The lives of four teenagers are altered forever. As anchor woman Diane Sawyer sets up the final episode of this sad story, she warns us of even a stranger twist. The parents of the murdered cheerleader visit one of the teenagers now in prison to offer him the gift of their forgiveness. "We must not let our hearts become bitter," say the weeping parents, "we must learn to forgive."

What is this national obsession with forgiveness? *The Courier Journal*, *The Wall Street Journal*, and *Readers Digest* have all recently carried articles concerning forgiveness. Could we be learning as a society that bitterness, hate, revenge, and rage are losers' games? No, forgiveness is never easy. It's just necessary!

Loving God, thank you for allowing us to seek your forgiveness. By this act, we can learn to forgive others. Amen.

Room for Error

In a *Peanuts* cartoon, Lucy is lecturing Charlie Brown on the facts of life. "Sooner or later, Charlie Brown, there is one thing you're going to have to learn. You reap what you sow! You get out of life exactly what you put into it, no more and no less."

Snoopy, who is listening to this conversation, stops to ponder. Then he runs off by himself lamenting, "I'd kind of like to see a little more margin for error."

When it comes to life, I'm with Snoopy. I'd like to see a little more margin for error. That's why I like words like forgiveness, grace, and mercy. They breathe new life into our sins and shortcomings. They remind us we are not locked into the prison of our past.

Forgiveness does not change the past; it forges a future. Grace does not solve all our problems, but it does remove the guilt that haunts us in the night. Mercy is the pardon we don't deserve, the break we never thought we would get.

While life leaves us accountable, we are wise to remember that life is also redeemable.

God of creation, we know you give us room for error in the choices we make in life. We ask that you continue to show us forgiveness and mercy. Thank you also for giving us your grace! Amen.

Confession

A thoughtful parent wrote this letter to his son who was going off to college.

"I seek your forgiveness for all the times I talked when I should have listened, got angry when I should have been patient, acted when I should have been delighted, scolded when I should have encouraged, criticized when I should have complimented, said no when I should have said yes and said yes when I should have said no. I often tried too hard, demanded too much, and mistakenly tried to mold you in my image rather than encouraging you to discover the person God made you to be. For this I am sorry. Love, Dad."

It's been said that confession is good for the soul. It is also essential for relationships. Forgiveness is the oil that lubricates the human machine. Without it all of life becomes hot and squeaky. So, how about it? Do you have relationships that could use the oil of forgiveness today?

Help me, Forgiving Savior, to find the words to show my love for those around me. I need and want to express my love for them, but I get too busy and become indifferent. Give me the courage and strength to accomplish this. Amen

Getting Even

A visitor to Yellowstone National Park discovered that bears were willing to share their food with only one animal. That animal was a skunk. With one swing of its powerful paw, the bear could have crushed the skunk. Instead, the bear let the striped intruder eat right along beside him. Evidently the bear had learned from previous experience the high cost of getting even.

Have you learned the high cost of getting even? While revenge is a natural human emotion, people are wise to count the cost before trying to settle the score. Revenge has led to an endless cycle of bloodshed in the Middle East. Revenge has torn families apart and alienated friends forever. Revenge has damaged communities and destroyed churches. Revenge is not sweet; it is apt to cause more stink than a skunk after its breakfast.

*God of us all, may we learn that revenge is not the answer.
Teach us to live in peace with one another.
We pray this in your Holy name. Amen*

Feud

After 125 years, the infamous feud between the Hatfields and the McCoys is officially over. On June 14, 2003, in Pikeville, Kentucky, sixty descendants of the original clan gathered to sign a document declaring an official end to more than a century of hatred and bloodshed. It all began in 1878 when Randolph McCoy accused one of the Hatfields of stealing a hog. It escalated into eleven deaths and endless court battles over timber rights and cemetery plots.

Now, the feud is officially over. Surrounded by state dignitaries, the descendants signed a peace treaty which read, "We do hereby and formally declare an official end to all hostilities implied, inferred, and real between the families, now and forevermore."

Well, how about it? Are there hostilities that need to cease and peace treaties that need to be signed between you and significant others? If the Hatfields and McCoys can do it, why can't we?

We let little disagreements grow into big arguments
that at times even turn into fights.
Dear Lord, give me wisdom to walk away when matters get out of
hand. Help me to know when to walk away! Amen.

Roy

For 69 years Roy lived in an institution for the mentally handicapped. Then, a few years ago he moved to L'Arche Daybreak Community, a place where the handicapped are treated with dignity and personal attention. Many people thought Roy would not make the adjustment. They were wrong. Within weeks this exuberant warmhearted man had friends eager to take him fishing or out for coffee. He delighted in the unlocked refrigerator, where he could have all he wanted to eat.

Roy could have been bitter about his past—all he had missed by his confinement. Instead, he chose to rejoice in all that he was discovering. Instead of lamenting yesterday, Roy embraced today and looked forward to tomorrow.

How are you dealing with the circumstances of your life? All of us have troubles to bear and challenges to face. But here's the truth: It's not what happens to us as much as what we do with what happens to us that makes the difference. Freedom is a state of mind as well as a set of circumstances.

Loving Savior, fill us with unending joy so that we can rejoice in our blessings and see goodness and love all around us regardless of our situation. Put a smile on our faces today and in the days to come. We give thanks in your name. Amen.

Revenge

In a classic experiment at Yale University, a group of people were told they were participating in important research regarding human behavior. They were then instructed to work a dial that was supposed to administer a shock to the person sitting beyond the window. Of course the person was actually an actor, who grimaced in great pain as the dial was turned. To the researchers huge surprise, 100% of the participants administered what they thought was an intense, painful shock to the actor behind the window.

What is this hunger in the human heart to inflict pain on another? Is it vengeance? Is it rage? Is it some craving to get even with another? It was Mahatma Gandhi who said, "If we live by the ethic of an eye for an eye and a tooth for a tooth, the world will soon be blind and toothless." Indeed it will. So let our justice be tempered by mercy, and our hurts find healing in time that all may taste and see that life can be good.

Merciful God, let there be mercy in our world to heal the pain and suffering. Help us to experience your love and remember that we are your children. And, let it begin with me! Amen.

Empowered Giving

The son of Lloyd LeBlanc was brutally murdered. As Mr. LeBlanc arrived in a cane field, with sheriff deputies to identify his son, the stunned father knelt by his boy and prayed the Lord's Prayer. When Lloyd came to the words, "Forgive us our trespasses as we forgive those who trespass against us," he paused and said, "Whoever did this, God, help me forgive them."

Forgiveness. It is an empowered form of giving. When we forgive the people who bring us pain, we step into the stream of healing grace. Forgiveness may not help the person who receives it. It never fails to help the person who gives it. Forgiveness fits faulty people.

"Forgiveness is a daily challenge," continues Mr. LeBlanc. "Each day I have to over come feelings of bitterness and revenge."

There's nothing easy or cheap about forgiveness. But believe me, it is well worth the price!

Dear Jesus, the Lord's Prayer teaches us, "to forgive those who have trespassed against us." Through the power of your redeeming grace, help us to practice forgiveness each and every day. Amen.

It's All Right

The most famous photo of the Vietnam War appeared June 1971 showing a small girl running naked down a road with an expression of unimaginable terror, her clothes burned off, her body scorched by napalm. U.S. army pilot John Plummer coordinated that raid and when he saw the picture he was knocked to his knees in shock and sorrow.

The years passed. Pham Thi Kim survived and moved to Toronto. Then in 1996, Kim was invited to speak at a Veterans Day observance in Washington. Plummer attended. During the speech Kim said, "If I could talk face to face with the pilot who dropped the bombs, I would tell him we cannot change history, but we should try to do good things for the present." That's when John Plummer slipped her a note saying, "I am the man."

Following the speech they met. Plummer fell into her arms sobbing, saying he was sorry. Kim replied "It's all right. I forgive."

God invented forgiveness as a remedy for a past that even he could not change. The time to find forgiveness is now.

Loving God, forgiveness has its beginning in our hearts.
Open our hearts to accept your love so that we might forgive others.
Amen.

Restlessness

Do you ever want to drop everything and start a whole new life? Such urges are surely among the most received and rejected of all human signals for change. There are, however, valid reasons for not doing what we sometimes impulsively feel the urge to try. As I look back over the big moves that I have considered but never made, I am grateful. Maybe I missed a few great opportunities for adventure, but "staying put" and "sticking tight" have enabled me to take another trip, an interior travel through the geography of my private self. There, I discovered truths and enjoyed scenery never available to those who are content to just move on. So the next time you sense that drive to drop everything and start a whole new life, don't move out, move in.

For down in the human heart, crushed by the tempter, feelings lie buried that grace can restore. We can know ourselves. We can forgive ourselves. We can find the grace to carry on. We can experience peace that passes all understanding. So, make a positive move today. Become friends with your inner self.

Good Shepherd, lead me in my life's journey so that I can find a meaningful destination. Show me the path to travel that will allow me to experience the "peace that passes all understanding." Amen.

Identity and Values

Human Value

From a chemical point of view, humanity is not worth very much. The average size person contains enough fat to make seven bars of soap, enough iron to make a medium size nail, enough lime to cover a twenty by forty foot lawn, enough phosphorus to make 2,200 match tips, enough magnesium for a single dose, and enough potassium to explode a toy cannon. Sold at current market prices, a person is worth less than $20.

Is materialism all there is? Of course not. Red or Yellow, black or white, people are precious in God's sight. And we are wise to treat humans with similar high esteem. Life is sacred. People are holy. We are called to tread softly and speak reverently in the presence of others. No money can buy the smile of a child. No stock can replace the value of a friend. No estate can restore the wisdom of a parent. From intimate friends to strangers on the street, we are wise to value human beings.

O Lord, you have made us in your image; may we value human life and learn to live in harmony with one another. Amen.

Carl Sandburg

Poet Carl Sandburg once said, "There is an eagle in me that wants to soar and a hippopotamus in me that wants to wallow in the mud."

Isn't that true of us all? Deep within our souls there exists the potential for greatness and the temptation to laziness. Which will we follow? Ah, that is the question!

We human beings need not be addicted to situations or enslaved to circumstances. We have wings like an eagle. We have the ability to rise toward the sky. We can overcome our difficulties. We can pursue our potential. We can dream dreams and dare to fulfill them. We can soar.

Or we can wallow in the mud like a hippopotamus. We can endure the day in the dirt. We can complain about the things that are and resent the things that might have been. We can exist instead of live. We can shrink our world to a single pleasure that doesn't even bring satisfaction any more.

God did not make us to wallow in some mud hole like a hippopotamus. God made us to spread our wings and fly!

Father God, you gave us free will and we must make our own choices. Give us strength though to seek goodness and live a life of purpose. Amen.

The Lion King

The Lion King was a roaring hit. This Broadway musical with its stunning costumes and powerful music tells the story of Simba, the lion cub who hesitates to take his place of leadership in the circle of life. The plot is profoundly true. Shame and guilt, along with an attitude of hakuna matata—"don't worry; be happy"—can distract us from our true selves. It is easy to forget who we are and why we are here. Quite often it takes a funky priest like Rafiki or a time of reflection by the still water to bring us back to our true purpose for being. Thank God we are not destined to live among the wart hogs and hyenas. We can become what we were created to be.

So in human life, never settle for anything less than your personal best. There is good we can do, a contribution we can make, a better life we can live. So, let us neither defer it nor neglect it. Let us take our full potential and live into it for the glory of God and the good of people.

Dear Lord, help me to strive to do my very best every day so that I might live a life of glory to God and for the good of others. Amen.

Be All You Can Be

Martin Luther King Jr. constantly encouraged people to be all they can be. "Not everyone is born a Cadillac," he said in a sermon, "but a Ford can get into places where a Cadillac won't fit."

"Sweep streets so well that all the host of heaven and earth will have to pause and say, 'Here lived a great street sweeper who did his job well,'" Luther added.

"If it falls to your lot to be a street sweeper, sweep streets like Michelangelo painted pictures, sweep streets like Beethoven composed music. Sweep streets like Shakespeare wrote poetry. Sweep streets so well that all the host of heaven and earth will have to pause and say: Here lived a great street sweeper who swept his job well.

> "If you can't be a pine on the top of the hill
> Be a scrub in the valley— but be
> The best little scrub on the side of the hill.
> Be a bush if you can't be a tree.
> If you can't be a highway, just be a trail
> If you can't be the sun be a star
> It isn't by size that you win or fail
> Be the best of whatever you are."

We all have different gifts and talents. When it comes to ability, people are not equal. However, what we do with what we are makes all the difference.

Thank you Heavenly Father for life. Help me to use my talents and abilities to be the best I can be. Amen.

Identity

Who are you, and can you prove it? That seems to be an important question in our terror filled world. At airports and department stores, on highways and ordinary days, we are constantly being asked for proof of our identity. My wife and I were flying to Cincinnati for a wedding. It was a one day trip so my wife didn't see a need for a purse. At the ticket counter she had no proof of her identity. No amount of pleading got her through the gate. We learned the hard way to never leave home without your identity.

Whether or not it is clear to us, we have a God-given identity. He knits us together in our mother's womb and claims us at birth as His very own. We are children of the universe, no less than the moon and the stars. We have a right to be here. Isn't it about time we remembered who we are? We are God-designed and God-loved and God-owned. From God, we came, and to God we shall return. So claim your God given identity, and be ready at all times to prove who you are!

God of Creation, help us always to be mindful of who we are — children of God. Amen.

Werner Center

The Werner Center for the Performing Arts at Ohio State University is built with staircases that lead to nowhere and pillars that hang suspended from the ceiling. When a visitor asked the reason for such odd architectural design, he was told the building was designed to reflect life itself. Has a feeling of suspension and stairs that lead to nowhere pervaded your philosophy of life?

I hope not! In spite of the pervasive pessimism that saturates post modern culture, we have reason to be hopeful and positive. Life is valuable. Creation is beautiful. Relationships can be rewarding. Work can be meaningful. Why settle for quiet desperation when vibrant inspiration is as close as a walk in the woods or a visit to a house of worship? You are a child of God, no less than the moon and the stars; you have a good reason for being here.

Life is a blessing. Teach us, O Lord, how to enjoy creation so we will know how to live. Amen.

Sea Biscuit

"You don't throw a life away just because it's banged up a bit." That's what trainer Tom Smith said to owner Charles Howard when asked why he would spend so much time nursing an injured horse to health in the touching movie *Sea Biscuit*.

What applies to horses applies to people too. In our throw-away society, we are tempted to toss people in the garbage when they fail to make it in the world. We find ourselves considering laws against street people because their presence is bad for business. We put the elderly on a shelf in forgotten places when they cease to be productive.

Maybe it's time to pose a question: Is our worth as human beings determined by our usefulness? Are we only as valuable as our number of wins in life? Is productivity synonymous with purpose? If we shouldn't throw away an animal just because it gets banged up a bit, how much more should we protect the worth of every human being?

Every person is a child of the universe. They have a right to be here. They deserve our respect, our assistance, and our deepest devotion.

Dear Jesus, you have taught us to love our fellow man as we love ourselves. So many times we fail to do so. Renew in our hearts the love for every human being. Amen.

Popularity

Marvin Griffin ran for Governor of Georgia back in the sixties. His campaign strategy was to serve barbecue dinners throughout the state. People loved it. As many as 10,000 people would show up at one of Marvin's political barbecues. But when it came time to vote, Marvin lost the election by a decisive majority. At a news conference held after the election, Marvin said, "It's obvious they liked Marvin's barbecue better than they liked Marvin."

Have you discovered that people like what you can do for them much more than they like you? As long as you are meeting their needs, fulfilling their wishes, sustaining their desires, you are company worth keeping. That may not translate to support, however, when the chips are down.

So never judge your self-worth by opinion polls. You are much more than another's opinion. You are a child of God. And no less than the moon and the stars, there is a purpose for your being here.

Dear Lord, help us to place our trust in you and not man alone.
We receive our worth from being a child of God.
Thanks be to God. Amen.

Silent Cal

President Calvin Coolidge was a man of few words. People nicknamed him "Silent Cal." One night at a state dinner, a lady was seated near the president at the head table. During the meal, she leaned over to Coolidge and whispered, "some of my friends bet me ten dollars you wouldn't say more than two words all evening." The president eyed her for a moment and tonelessly replied, "You lose."

In this era of political posturing, when everybody's talking and not many people are listening, I wonder if we could use some of Calvin Coolidge's reserve. It's been said that we humans have two ears and one mouth and therefore, by creation, were intended to listen twice as much as we speak. There is a difference between having to say something and having something to say.

Maybe that applies to our personal lives as well as politics. The hunger of the human heart is to be heard and understood. That, of course, requires active listening. Are we willing to be quick to listen and slow to speak with those who mean the most to us?

Help us O Lord, to listen to those we love and be slow to speak.
Teach us this simple act. Amen.

Problem or Solution

In the movie *Annie Hall*, Woody Allen tells the story about a man who goes to a psychiatrist complaining that his brother-in-law, who lives with him, thinks he is a chicken. "Describe his symptoms," said the doctor. "Maybe I can help."

"Well," said the man. "He cackles a lot, pecks at the rug and furniture, and makes nests in the corner."

"Sounds like a simple neurosis to me," replied the doc. "Bring him in, I think I can cure him completely."

"Oh no," exclaimed the man. "we wouldn't want that. We need the eggs."

When it comes to creating a better, healthier world, we must decide if we are part of the problem or part of the solution. Sometimes, we become so accustomed to things as they are and so dependent upon problems as they exist that any possibility for change is met with intense resistance. How dare people suggest we eat healthier, drive safer, pollute less, care more? We want things to be better but only if they do not affect our ways of thinking and living.

Lord, help us to accept change in our lives; help me to be part of the solution and not the problem. In your name we pray. Amen.

Example

Poet Mildred Ramsey reminds us that "While traveling on this road of life, you may be unaware that someone's coming on behind who'd follow you most anywhere."

People are watching us. It may be a child that you hardly see, or a true admirer or close employee. It may be a person you meet at church, or some close friend you leave in a lurch. Whatever the circumstances, we do not live private lives with the freedom to do as we please. We are accountable for our actions and responsible for our example.

You know, I'm glad about that. People will not remember the speeches we make. Most will not care about the rewards we receive. Even the work we accomplish will fade in importance with the passing of time. But the values we communicate to a child, and the ethics we demonstrate at work, and the spirit we embody in the routines of life will endure from generation to generation.

So live a life that really matters. It will make a difference to you and especially to others.

Help me Lord Jesus to live a life that makes a difference to others. Help my actions to be acceptable to you. Amen.

Jackpot

Mark Wayne Metcalf won 65 million dollars in a Powerball jackpot. He thought he'd finally have it made. What he had was a life of misery. He split the money with his wife, and they went their separate ways. He built a big, new house, but found himself isolated and alone. He found friends in the world of drugs for which he was arrested and served time in jail. He couldn't hold a steady job. Scam artists relieved Mark of his money. He died in his house, alone, and was not found for several days.

Do you have money, or does money have you? Most of us believe we would have it made if we could only strike it rich. Money does buy us things, but it does not give us life. Life is a gift. We can receive it with joy, live it with purpose, invest it in others, or squander it, waste it, and finally lose it. The choice is ours.

Mark Metcalf, shortly before his untimely death, supposedly said to a friend, "The money I won is the worst thing I could have wanted in life." What are you doing with the gifts you have received—especially the gift of life?

Everything we have is a gift from you, O God.
Help us receive gratefully and spend wisely. Amen.

Life Lessons

Brevity of Life

A university student asked Billy Graham to identify his greatest surprise about life? The renowned evangelist thought for a moment and replied, "the brevity of it all."

However we slice it, life is short. I know ninety-five year olds who have just begun to live and all kinds of friends who feel severely limited by twenty-four hour days. We invent multiple gadgets to save time, and still feel we never have enough time. For time, like an ever rolling stream, bears all who breathe away.

Wise people number their days. They do not lament their lack of time. They use their time in wonderful ways. They know time is a valuable gift, and they are determined to make the most of it.

What are you doing with the time of your life? Why not invest your time in things that last? Why not make the time for the things that matter? Why not seize each moment and spend each moment for the good of others and the betterment of a community that is sure to be around long after you are gone? It could extend your time to something longer than a single life.

Dear Lord Jesus, help us to use our time in meaningful ways that bring glory to you by serving others. Amen.

Pennies

I saw a penny on the sidewalk and thought how it was worth so little that nobody bothered to pick it up. It's hard to get half your two cents worth with a penny these days. But according to an article in *The Atlanta Journal Constitution*, a penny might be worth more than we think.

A penny increase in a case of Cokes would bring the company 45 million dollars a year. A one cent increase in the cost of jet fuel costs an airline 25 million dollars a year. A penny increase in the hourly wage of all Home Depot employees amounts to 6.5 million dollars a year. And, if Krispy Kreme increased the cost of each donut sold by one cent, their profits would go up 27 million dollars.

I meet a lot people whose feeling of self-worth is less than a penny. They've been bought, sold, and bartered in the marketplaces of life too many times. A very wise teacher once observed that two sparrows are sold for a penny. But people are worth much more than sparrows.

Maybe it's time to claim your real value.

Dear Jesus, you have told us we are loved children of God. Help us to accept this love into our lives. Amen.

Curves

Has life thrown you a curve lately? Major league baseball batters must learn to hit curve balls. They likely prefer pitches thrown down the middle, but that seldom happens. It's curve balls, sinker balls, knuckle balls, high balls, low balls, coming across the plate. To make it in the majors, great batters must learn to hit whatever comes at them.

Life throws curves, too. If we had it our way, we'd ask for slow pitches and sure hits. Instead, unexpected curves cause us to strike out. While we can't control the pitcher, we can improve the batting.

So, the next time life throws you a curve, don't complain, "Unfair" to the umpire in the sky. Hang in there. Practice. L.earn from strikeouts, study, and listen. In time, you will discover a great truth. Curve balls can be hit for home runs, too.

Loving God, strengthen us and sustain us when we face difficulties in life. Guide us through the ups and downs in our lives. In your Holy Name we pray. Amen.

I Know Just How You Feel

"I know just how you feel." I don't use that phrase much anymore, How about you? Well meaning comforters in life want to reassure every person in pain with "I know just how you feel." In fact, we never know exactly how another feels. Every life experience is intensely personal. At best, we are able to understand what we have truly experienced. Only then does compassion begin.

I pastored a mother once who backed a car over her baby. I could never grip the grief that mother felt at the death of her child. A few years later, the same thing happened to another family in that community. Only the family who had been there already had the adequate capacity to understand.

Until we've walked a mile in another's shoes, like them who have been criticized or abused, known disease, distress, or death, and found at those very doors something more—then, and only then, dare we look another in the eye, and say "I know just how you feel."

Teach us compassion and understanding. Help us to realize that you and only you are God. Amen.

After a While

Author Veronica Shoffstall, summarized the learning of her life in a simple statement entitled *After a While*. In it, she says,

> "After a while you learn the subtle difference between holding a hand and chaining a soul. And you learn that love doesn't mean leaning, and company doesn't mean security. After a while you learn that kisses are not contacts and presents aren't promises. And you begin to accept your defeats with your head up and your eyes open. After a while you learn that you really can endure, you really are strong, and you really do have worth."

Life can be a great teacher. Even at the University of Hard Knocks we can learn lessons that last a lifetime and dramatically alter our actions the next time. We are not destined to live in the same ruts, wrestle with the same weakness, or endure the same pain forever. We can do better. After a While, can become wiser.

Dear wise and wondrous God, as we experience life, may you be our teacher and may we learn life's lessons from you. Amen.

Stick Shifts

"Lesson number 109" in Jackson Browne's little instruction book on life is, "Know how to drive a stick shift." I thought about that as I listened to my administrative assistant's concerns about driving her son's car on slick roads. Like any good parent, she had traded her comfortable SUV for a very used stick shift sports car, so her son could make a trip out of town. The good-willed and good-intentioned gesture, however, left her more than a little anxious. She had not driven a stick shift in a very long time, and did not feel very comfortable with all the clutch control required to navigate city traffic. Love and good will created its own dilemma.

Isn't that always the case? We do not live life automatically. Although cruise control saves me some speeding tickets, I realize heavy traffic calls for me to take charge of the brake and accelerator to determine my own destiny. The car is not going to navigate itself.

So how are you doing on the roads of life? Have you the knowledge and confidence to slow down, gear down, make turns that assure your safe arrival? Smart people are prepared to drive a stick shift, for sometimes they have to.

Help us, Lord Jesus, to navigate the roads of life. Teach us how to handle the twists and turns in life so we may reach our destination. Amen.

Airplane

Four men were traveling in an airplane. They included a pastor, a business executive, a boy scout, and the pilot. Somehow the plane lost power and started down.

"We'll have to jump," explained the pilot, "but there are only three parachutes. I have a young family and if I were killed they would really miss me." With that, the pilot grabbed a parachute and jumped.

The business executive spoke next. "Many people think I'm the smartest man in all the world," he explained. "If I were to go down with this plane, the world would suffer a great loss. I'm taking a parachute too," he said as he grabbed for one and jumped.

The pastor looked at the scout. "Son," he said, "you are young, I am old. You take the parachute, I'll ride it out."

But the scout replied, "Relax Reverend, the smartest man in all the world just jumped with a back pack instead of a parachute."

There are smart people going down all over the world that have grabbed a backpack in greed and missed the parachute of God's grace. The sudden stop will reveal the difference.

Dear God, help us to accept your unconditional love and be embraced in your arms of grace and forgiveness. Amen.

Dead Man

Did you hear about the man who was convinced he was dead? He just laid around every day on the living room sofa saying, "I'm dead. I'm not living anymore."

Well, all his friends came around trying to convince him he was still alive. They tried humor. They thought they could tease him out of it. But the man insisted, "I'm dead. No two ways about it; I'm gone."

One friend decided to reason with him. "Do dead men bleed?" he asked.

"No," said the dead man. "The blood coagulates."

The friend whipped out his knife, slashed the "dead" man's finger, and of course, the blood came pumping out. The dead man looked at his bleeding finger a moment and said, "Well, I'll be darned, dead men do bleed!"

That's my story, and I'm stickin to it. Well I've stuck to some stories too long, how about you? Some prejudices, opinions, thoughts, and expressions are worth changing. A change of mind, like a change of heart, can open new possibilities of life. Try it, you might like it.

Teach us, O Lord, how to live. Help us to overcome our prejudices, opinions and thoughts so we might live as you would have us to do. Amen.

Waiting

The average American, in a lifetime, will spend five years waiting in line, two years returning phone calls, eight months opening junk mail and six months staring at traffic lights. In spite of modern technology, the first sign we often see on the computer screen is "please wait," and every phone customer is put on hold.

Do you wait with purpose or perplexity? "To wait, or not to wait," is not the question. The only question is *how* we wait. According to statistics, the cost of running red lights is seven billion dollars a year. The average time saved is fifty seconds. Traffic jams are seldom solved by the blowing of horns. Cursing does not seem to get customer representatives on the phone more quickly. However, kindness does dissolve wrath, and prayer is a good way to wait through long delays.

Great Teacher, teach me kindness and caring, and give me patience through the power of daily prayer. Amen.

Focus

I picked up the pictures from the developer. They were prints of a significant family event. As I hurried to view them, I discovered they were blurred, fuzzy, and not very good. I took them with a new camera, but I discovered, too late, that I failed to properly set its focus.

I sometimes have that trouble with life too, How about you? When life is out of focus, the priorities of living become fuzzy. Unfocused, we try to do everything and wind up accomplishing nothing.

I like to think of worship as a way to focus life. In the presence of God, I discover who I am and what I need to become. Trivial things pass away. Important values become clear.

Thank you, God, for your church. Grant us wisdom through the power of worship to see life more clearly. Amen.

Evil One

The woman from Georgetown, Kentucky, who encountered a cougar on a Saturday evening stroll outside her home, reminded me of this story.

Two explorers were on a jungle safari when suddenly a ferocious lion jumped in front of them. "Keep calm," the first explorer whispered. "Remember what we read in the book on wild animals? If you stand perfectly still and look the lion in the eye, he will turn and run."

"Sure," replied the second explorer. "You've read the book, and I've read the book, but has the lion read the book?"

Fear is a friend of reindeer, rabbit, and smart people. We must realize that everyone does not play by the same rules in this game of life. The evil one, like a roaring lion, prowls about seeking whom he may devour. As psychiatrist Scott Peck puts it in his book, *The People of the Lie*, "I know Satan exists. I have met it." When we come face to face with evil, we will be wise to find a way of escape.

Lord, lead us not into temptation and deliver us from evil. Amen.

Work

"I'm a great believer in luck," wrote Thomas Jefferson, "And the harder I work the more luck I have."

In our something-for-nothing kind of world, we could use a new wave of Jefferson thinking. Our national heroes were not jackpot winners. Even the prize of a new country presented problems and challenges only conquered by productive hard work. They met those challenges with focused minds and faithful imaginations. They took what they wanted and paid for it: some with their lives, and all with their sacred honor.

What has happened to the value of hard work? Has "luck" replaced work as American's favorite four letter word? Life does not owe us a living. We owe our living to life. We need responsible, honest, hard-working people who are determined to make the world a better place, one day at a time.

Dear God, thank you for the vision and hard work of those who have gone before us. May we strive to honor you by always doing our best work. Amen.

Empty

Have you noticed how our cars talk to us these days? They tell us to fasten our seat belts, close our doors, check under the hood, and put air in our tires. Most of all, they tell us when we are low on gas. There is a red line on the gauge. When we push toward empty, a light comes on and a bell rings. It rings out a warning to pull over and refuel. Even the best of cars stall when they run out of gas.

People have a way of running out of gas too. Empty is a spiritual, physical, mental, and emotional condition calling for immediate attention and concrete action. Empty leaves us feeling separated from God, unable to cope, confused about priorities, and generally exhausted. People who ignore the warnings are sure to stall on the roads of life.

So the next time you are running on fumes, pull over and stop at an appropriate refueling station. Take good care of yourself physically. Feed your soul spiritually. Find a good mental and emotional balance. It could make all the difference in your life.

Help me, O Lord, to remember to be both physically and spiritually healthy in order to handle life's problems. We ask it in your name. Amen.

Peace

Cards

Every Christmas, our mailboxes are flooded with cards. People we seldom see send seasonal greetings. Friends near and far make contact by mail. Many cards contain messages of hope and pictures of peace. Pine trees stand amid smooth snowdrifts unmarked by footprints or snowmobiles. A mountain lake will mirror tall peaks, blue skies and soft fluffy clouds. A colorful sunset will light the sky, or a country church will remind us of days gone by.

Have you noticed most of these peaceful settings portray no pictures of people? Are they trying to say peace without people is possible? But, put people in it—well, that's another matter.

People do disturb our peace. People forced to live together before they are fit to live with each other: that's our human predicament. Yet the peace on earth we proclaim this season of the year, is not some hideaway hill undisturbed by human form. It is the presence of God in the thick and thin of human relationships, touching us gently with amazing grace.

Creator, may the love of Jesus Christ bring peace into our lives so we may be able to reach out to others. Amen.

Teenagers

According to the 2001 Roper Youth Report, more teenagers head to church in any given week than surf the web, see a movie, hang out at parties, or visit the mall. In fact, church going increased seven percent over the previous year. Fifty-three percent of teenagers ranked religion and spirituality among their top personal interests. Fifty-eight percent said church and religious groups are important influences on their moral values.

There is a spiritual hunger in America of fast growing proportions. People of all ages are searching for meaning and purpose, for a life that really matters. There is a difference between making a living and making a life. We can't build enough houses, make enough money, and travel enough places to make us internally peaceful. Peace is a result of soul work. Our souls are restless until they find their rest in God

So whatever your age or stage of life, isn't it about time you found peace with God? A connection with the eternal will stabilize the temporal and help your most difficult circumstances fall into place.

We cannot live our lives just for today, merciful God.
You put within us a spiritual hunger that must be fed by
a connection with believers and a peace in knowing you. Amen.

Tea Bags

As I made myself a cup of tea the other day, I thought how people are a lot like tea bags. You never know their real strength until they are thrown into hot water. A tea bag resting in a box is powerless, useless, and tasteless. But, put that same tea bag in a cup of boiling water, and watch its instant strength go to work. Clear water is transformed into tasty tea, useful enough to quench a thirst, fine enough to serve your most honored guest.

I don't particularly like being in hot water. Hot water can hurt you, burn you, or even blister you for life. I prefer the pleasant streams of peace and calm to the bubbling steam of troubling discussions and heated debate. Yet, when thrown into hot water like a tea bag, we will do well to transform the boiling liquid into tasty refreshment.

When we are thrown into the turmoil of life, give us strength to endure so we may enjoy the peace and calm that comes from the love of our Lord and Savior. Amen.

Deciding What Matters

"You got to know when to hold 'em, know when to fold 'em, know when to walk away, and know when to run." There's something about those lyrics from that old Kenny Rogers' ballad that rings true to life. Day by day, in multiple ways, we decide the battles to face and the conflicts to avoid.

There are things worth fighting for. There are principles and values that deserve our defense and need our support. There is a time to take a strong stand and determine whatever the cost to do no other, but not always.

Choose your battles wisely. Is it really worth the fuss to fume over which movie to watch tonight? Does a small scratch on your car really warrant a suit in small claims court? If kids insist on cutting across your yard, does the damage deserve a confrontation?

Certainly, we must decide, but more and more, I am deciding not to sweat the small stuff. Some fights are just not worth winning. And the peace that passes understanding gives greater joy than all the commotion of conflict.

Gracious God, help me to see what really matters in my life—my family, my health, my faith—and let the things I cannot change go. In your name we pray. Amen.

Why?

Why? Why? The world is asking "why?" In light of a shooting rampage that kills three teens and injures five more, sensible people are asking, "why?"

We'd like to blame the family, but they are too much like us. We'd like to blame the devil, but that's too frightening for most of us. Could it be the media? Maybe movies are at fault. Inquiring minds want to know, as if to know is the road to control. If we only knew the reasons, we could be safe for all seasons. Ah, that is the dilemma of human grandiosity. We think we are masters of our own fate and captains of our own souls.

While some see things as they are and ask, "why?" I tend to dream of things that never were and ask, "why not?" Why not better gun control? Why not moral education? Why not outrage at the ethic of "anything goes?" Why not return to religious values of right and wrong? The puzzle of tragedy may never be solved. But it is lack of will more than lack of knowledge that causes our greatest harm.

Dear Lord, we want answers to our questions, and we want results from our prayers. But so often we don't find the whys or get the answers. You are the God of creation and the answers will come in your time, not ours. Let us remember that. Amen.

Wishbone

In a *Peanuts* cartoon, Lucy explains the old wishbone game to Charlie Brown. "Whoever breaks off the biggest piece gets to make a wish," says Lucy. "And I wish for a new doll, a bicycle, four new sweaters, new saddle shoes, a wristwatch and about a $100.00."

Charlie Brown replies, "I wish for a long life for all my friends, peace in the world, and great advances in science and medicine."

With that, Lucy throws away the bone in disgust and says, "You seem to have a knack for spoiling everything."

What are your greatest wishes? Are you longing for more clothes to fill your closet or more comfort for others? Does your wish list have yourself right in the middle of it or does it hold great dreams for the good of society? The things we wish for are likely the things we will work for. If there is to be peace on our streets, hope for our sick, faith in our nation, and love for the world, we must wish for it in our hearts and work for it with all our lives.

God of all, help me to wish for those things that will make a difference and give me the ability to make it happen. Amen.

Baseball

A little boy with baseball cap in place, ball and bat in hand, went out to play in the backyard. "I'm the greatest baseball player in the world," exclaimed the boy as he pitched the ball in the air, swung at it and missed.

The boy pitched the ball in the air a second time and said, "I'm the greatest baseball player ever." Once more he swung and missed.

He tried it a third time saying, "I'm the greatest baseball player who ever lived." For a third time, he swung and missed.

Down, but not out, the boy dropped his bat and said, "Wow, what a pitcher."

The soul is dyed the color of its thoughts. We can alter life by altering our attitudes. We can approach life with fear, frustration, and failure. Or, we can approach life with confidence, courage, and commitment. The choice is ours. We may not be good at everything, but we are good for something. So let us take that something and do it well for the good of others as well as ourselves.

God of our play and our work, help us to be like the little boy playing baseball. He took what was bad and saw good in it. Help us to make a difference with a positive attitude. Amen.

Living Forever

I saw this statement on a personal bulletin board. "I intend to live forever—so far, so good." Can you say that?

Brad Paisley's hit song suggests, "When we get to where we're going, there'll be only happy tears. In time we will learn to shed the sins and sorrows that we've carried all these years."

Do you believe that? Even some religious people would have us dread tomorrow, fear death, worry about eternity. My religion does not cause me to do that. I believe tomorrow will be better than today. I have the fervent faith that life on the other side will be even greater than the life I enjoy here. I know my mind is far too limited to grasp the height and depth, the breadth and width, and the experience or the expanse of eternity. I do intend to live forever.

And, I can honestly say, "So far, so good." No life is perfect. All of us struggle and shed some tears. Yet, by grace, we learn the love that overcomes our greatest fears. Let us live fully, all our years.

O Lord, let us live our lives fully each and every day knowing that Jesus Christ died on the cross for us so we might have eternal life.
Amen.

Vengeance

A cartoonist portrayed the never ending cycle of vengeance this way: A boss yells at an employee. The employee walks in the door yelling at his wife. The wife, standing at the kitchen sink, begins to yell at the child. The child responds by kicking the family dog. The dog goes out the door and uses the bathroom on the boss's lawn.

We live in an age of personal and international revenge. The human urge to pay others back for the harm they have done is raging like a forest fire. It shows its ugly face in the Middle East, on America's streets, and in the close quarters of family life. Who is going to break the cycle?

Perhaps a place to start is to take our anger to the Lord and leave it there. We all need a place to dump our hurts, lest we internalize them and let them harden into personal bitterness. Fear of injustice prompts us to take matters into our own hands where we function as judge, jury, and jailhouse. We are hardly qualified for such Divine service.

Merciful Savior, help us remember that vengeance is yours.
Help us remember to let you be the judge and jury rather than us.
Amen.

Jesus Weeps

Out in Oklahoma City, across the street from the Murrah Federal Building where 168 people were killed by a terrorist bomb, St. Joseph Catholic Church has erected a tall statue of a white robed Christ. He is standing with his back to the memorial, his head bowed, and one hand is covering his face. There, in the midst of death and terror, Christ is weeping.

Wherever innocent people suffer, Jesus weeps. When soldiers are killed in Iraq, and children are neglected by parents, Jesus weeps. When teenagers get hooked on drugs, and families fall apart, Jesus weeps. When the elderly are abandoned, and spouses are abused, Jesus weeps. He weeps over what is and what might have been. God is not watching us from a distance. God is standing with us in the shadows.

So let us be about the business of breaking the cycle of hate. Let us take up the cause of peace. Let us work for the good of others and the glory of God.

Let us break the cycle of hate, loving Jesus, and let it start with me.
Amen.

Violence

"If we live by the sword, we die by the sword!" Could that old proverb be true? Day by day, we abhor the violence in our city. The numbers alone are staggering. How long can we run to another part of town for safety, fooling ourselves that crime will not follow us? Murder is everybody's menace. It is time for the violence to stop.

Police can help. Politicians can assist. But something deeper must transpire in the human spirit for people to melt their weapons of destruction into tools for gardening. Human life must be valued. Gun control must increase. Community must be recovered. People helping people must become the norm of life. We cannot glorify violence and greed and continue to be surprised that people practice it. If we live by the sword, we are likely to die by the sword. Is it not time to put our swords away? Let us live together as brothers and sisters lest we perish apart as fools.

Dear Jesus, if we continue to live by the sword we will bring destruction on ourselves and our country. Help us to value human life and live together as brothers and sisters of Christ. Amen.

Perserverance

The Big Race

The Kentucky Derby may be the greatest two minutes in sports, but you and I are running a race that's bigger than life. Some call it a rat race, but it doesn't have to be. From the cradle to the grave we have an opportunity to cross the finish line for a crown that is bigger than life.

One successful racer put it this way: This one thing I do – forgetting those things which are behind, and straining toward what is ahead, I press on toward the goal to win the prize God has prepared for me.

It's easy to be a starter, but are you a "sticker to"? It's easy enough to begin a race. It's harder to see it through. Races are seldom determined in the flashy starts or fancy finishes. Its the silent plodding through the mud slinging of the back stretch that makes us or breaks us. When the cheering starts have faded and the finish line is not in sight, have the you courage, the stamina, the determination, and the faith, to be a winner too.

Sustainer, Redeemer, be with us in the race of life and guide us toward the finish line—life eternal—prepared for us by Christ Jesus. Amen.

Happiness

In a *Peanuts* cartoon, Charlie Brown comes up to Linus and says, "You know what? Yesterday I was almost happy. For one brief shining moment, I thought I was winning in the game of life. Then I discovered there was a flag on the play!"

In the big game of life, it often feels like one yard forward and ten yards backward. Life is hard on the scrimmage line. It's hard for everyone. There are tackles, collisions, clips, and personal fouls. There are turnovers, trip ups, fumbled passes, and missed field goals. No wonder Americans love football. It looks a lot like life.

Winners on every field are people who overcome lost yardage. They stay in the game when there's a flag on the play. Little by little they find their way to the goal line. Consider this: Even in football you get four tries to gain ten yards. Should we expect any less on the field of life?

Dear Lord, help us to see you in all circumstances. When we face tough situations, help us to remember that the Holy Spirit is living and working in us. Amen.

Edison

As a child, Thomas Edison was anything but brilliant. One teacher described him as "addled." In reality, he was a slow, systematic thinker who never relied on luck. He had a thousand experiments that failed before he succeeded in inventing the light bulb. Success, according to Thomas Edison, was "one percent inspiration and 99% perspiration."

The story of Edison is repeated often. The best students in college are not always the most brilliant. They are focused persons who are determined to get an education. The most successful employees are not always the brightest minds on the block. They are committed persons who are willing to concentrate on the task until it is completed.

Intelligence is a gift distributed in varied proportions to human beings. Wisdom is the creative use of that gift. Wise people are able to focus their energies on a specific goal until the task is accomplished — even if it takes a thousand attempts.

Dear Lord, give us wisdom and the strength of character to remain focused on obtaining our goals in life. Amen.

Keeping On

"I'm not going back to school tomorrow," laments a certain family member, propping up his feet in the family den. "The teachers don't like me, the children don't like me, even the cafeteria workers talk behind my back."

"You will go back to school tomorrow," comes a voice from across the room. "You are six feet tall. You're 50 years old. Besides, you are the principal. You're paid to go."

Who of us, at one time or another, has not felt like skipping life tomorrow? The work is too hard. The demands are too many. The rewards are too few.

But come morning, there remain compelling reasons to return. Life is a trust. Time is limited. Responsibilities save us from worthlessness.

Most of all, God is there, transforming duty into design, helping us see the beauty of the forest in the midst of the trees. Accountability is one of life's most personal affirmations. You are needed and responsible. Thank God.

Thank you, Heavenly Designer, for teaching me how to live and giving me the strength to accept my responsibilities. Amen.

Smart People

Rushing through an airport to catch a plane, I was sweating and puffing along when I looked to my right and saw a man pass me by, walking half as fast as I. He was on the moving sidewalk that I had missed in my push to get ahead.

Traveling the roads of life, as well as the corridors of an airport, we should often try smarter instead of harder. There is wind beneath our wings, power under our feet, and wisdom for our journey closer than we imagine or realize. Smart people use all their resources.

So what are you facing today? Is it a mountain too steep to climb, a schedule impossible to keep, a task too tough to complete? Try smarter instead of harder. Before rushing forward with little thought or imagination, look around you and within you. Help may be closer than you think. Support may be nearer than you perceive. Most of all remember that great promise from the Bible. "I can do all things through Christ who strengthens me."

O God, you comfort us in our grief and lift us up in our despair. Thank you for the great hope we find in our risen Savior. In Jesus name we pray. Amen.

Reality

Reality TV is everywhere these days. From *The Apprentice* to *Fear Factor*, from *The Bachelor* to *Survivor*, we are invited to watch people deal with challenges while a television camera covers their every move. Instant stars are born and producers love the ratings. But does reality TV have anything to do with reality? How many of us are likely to hear Donald Trump say, "You're fired?" What bachelor really has twenty women who can't wait to be his wife? Do you really want to eat worms for money, or live on an island stranded with people determined to have you eliminated? It all sounds more like fantasy than reality to me.

Reality is getting up every day and going to work at a routine job. Reality is a couple trying to stay connected while raising a family. Reality is serving your community for the good of the world.

So how are you surviving in the real world? Are you finding the courage to carry on, the commitment to hang in there, and the determination to leave the world a little better than you found it? Now there is reality worth talking about.

Dear Lord, thank you for giving us the strength and courage to live each day to the best of our abilities. Amen.

Failure

How do you handle failure? Have you thought about that? To fail or not to fail is not the question. The question is what to do with failure. Michael Jordan once said, "I've missed more than 9,000 shots in my career. I've lost almost 300 games. On 26 occasions, I've been entrusted to take the game winning shot, and I missed. I have failed over and over again in my life. And that is precisely why I succeeded."

No toddler walks the first time they try. Scientists postulate theories and design experiments which often fail. Yet, in failing they may learn more than if they had succeeded. Great motivators perfect the art of public speaking by trying and trying again. It's not failure but low aim that does us in.

And you know what? I would rather fail in a cause that someday will triumph than win in a cause that will someday fail.

Help me, Lord to deal with failure. Give me the will to succeed and the ability to be successful. Amen.

Retirement

Tucked between two high stacks of incoming mail, Ziggy, in a Tom Wilson cartoon, entertains this thought: "Only 13,958 days until retirement."

I suppose there are times when all of us would like to hang it up, let it go, forget about it, and flee to some solitary spot of non-responsibility. Life has a way of piling up, becoming demanding, and leaving us with little room to peek out from behind the stacks.

When the going got tough, the ancient author of Psalms wanted to fly away like a bird into the mountains, find security in the isolation of the hills. Likewise, we conjure up get-away weekends and forget-it-all Fridays. Sometimes, like Ziggy, we count the days until retirement.

Escape, however, seldom improves our situation. Daydreaming does not dissolve the pile of unanswered mail. We even return from vacation to discover that it's all still waiting for us. So instead of slumbering at you desk with one long sigh, keep plugging at the pile one piece at a time.

Dear Lord, we live each day with thoughts on tomorrow.
Help us to be focused on the day and let tomorrow take care of itself.
We give thanks and praise to you. Amen.

Greener Grass

Author Robert Fulghum reminds us that the grass is not, in fact, "always greener on the other side of the fence. Fences have nothing to do with it. Grass is greener where it is watered." Have you thought about that?

Throughout life many of us are constantly looking for a better opportunity, a bigger break, or a greater chance to have it made. We spend our lives enviously looking over the fence hoping to graze in greener pastures. Maybe we could better use our time watering and fertilizing the grass where we are. Opportunity comes to those who have eyes to see and determination to follow the possibilities that lie before them. Big breaks often come in the form of little breaks that are maximized to their full potential. Being faithful over a few things has a way of growing into challenges of larger things.

So bloom where you are planted. Make the most of every moment. Give today all you've got. Be not anxious about tomorrow for tomorrow will have enough worries of its own.

Loving Father, teach us to have faith and to put our trust in you.
You have promised us eternal life.
In the name of Jesus Christ we pray. Amen.

Persistence Pays

When it comes to riding a bicycle, you can either keep pedaling, get off, or fall over. I suspect the bicycle principle applies to other parts of life as well. Persistence pays.

Thomas Edison held 1093 patents, still the record. He guaranteed productivity by giving himself, and his assistants idea quotas. His own personal quota was one minor invention every 10 days and one major invention every six months. Bach wrote a cantata every week, even when he was sick or exhausted. Mozart produced more than 600 pieces of music. Wesley wrote more than 6,000 hymns. Einstein is best known for his paper on relativity, but he published 248 other papers as well. Scientists conduct a lot more bad experiments than successful ones. And who of us in the great game of life, are lucky enough to get it right the first time?

If at first you don't succeed try, try, and try again. Keep on peddling; it beats the alternatives of quitting or falling.

Help us, dear Lord, to be persistent in the things we do knowing we may not always be right each time. Let us strive to be our best. Amen.

Life by the Inch

When racing reaches fever pitch in our community, I am reminded of that sign that used to hang over the track where I worked out. The sign said, "Life by the yard is hard. Life by the inch is a cinch." That's one way to say the longest journey begins with a single step.

Is there a long road stretching before you now? Maybe you are graduating from college and ready to tackle the corporate maze of things. Maybe you're a young mother burdened with diapers and dirty clothes. Maybe you're recently married, wondering if you can build a home out of a beautiful wedding. Life may have you facing a mountain, a mountain too steep to climb. It's then we need to pray, "Lord help me please, to take this situation one step at a time."

Step by step, life is manageable. Inch by inch, its a cinch. It takes superman qualities to leap tall buildings. It takes human determination to climb by the stairs, one step at time.

Dear steadfast and loving God, help me take one step at a time when faced with life's problems that seem overwhelming. Amen.

Outside the Box

Have you seen the cartoon featuring a man holding his pet cat, pointing to the kitty litter box, and saying firmly, "Never, ever, think outside the box." What is good for cats may not be so good for people. Creativity belongs to those who have the courage to think outside the box. Have you the vision to see outside the norm and beyond the ordinary?

Charles H. Duell, director of the U.S. patent office back in 1899, supposedly said, "Everything that can be invented has already been invented." In the meantime, others were obviously dreaming of things that did not exist and improving things that seemed impossible.

So there are two kinds of people who populate the earth. There are those who see things as they are and ask, "Why?" And there are those who dream of things that never were and ask, "Why not?" God has planted into the minds of people the ability to solve most of our problems, if we will only think outside the box.

Dear Lord, help me to seek your will in all I do so I may truly see the possibilities that exist for me. Amen.

Relationship with God

Personal Transformation

A person on their death bed had this to say about life: "When I was young and free my imagination had no limits, and I dreamed of changing the world. As I grew older and wiser, I discovered the world would not change, so I shortened my sights and decided to change my country. But it, too, seemed unmovable. Later in life, I went on a mission to change my family, those closest to me, but they would have none of it.

"Here on my deathbed, I have made a radical discovery. If only I had changed myself then, by example, my family would have been different. From their inspiration and encouragement, my country would have been a better place and who knows; even the world may have changed.

"I am only one. I cannot do everything. But still, I can do something. Because I cannot do everything, I will not refuse to do the something that I can do."

Transformation begins as an inside job. When we determine to be the very best that we can be, we start a minor ripple that could lead to a world revolution.

Dear God, help us to understand how our attitudes and choices affect what happens in the world around us. Amen.

Lease on Life

In a Tom Wilson cartoon, Ziggy is seeking assistance from a mortgage broker. As the receptionist asks Ziggy how she may help him, Ziggy replies, "Actually I'm looking for a new lease on life."

Well aren't we all? Over time, our lease on life seems to run out, fade, even end. What seemed like a good deal in the beginning is laced with questions now. Family is harder than we thought it would be. Work is not as rewarding as we hoped it would be. Disappointments pile up like dents on cars or wear on carpet, which prove to be costly in the end. We find ourselves needing a new lease on life.

Here's the good news. The God who created us in the first place can make us new. We can begin again. We can trade in an old life, dented and spotted and receive a new one all unblotted. We can get a new lease on life. It may call for change, but the change will be worth it. It could even be costly, but the product is priceless. You are valuable and precious in God's sight. So let him renew your lease on life.

Dear Heavenly Father, grant us the grace and strength to keep looking beyond our present hardships to the glorious future you are preparing for us. Amen.

ABC's of Prayer

In A Hank Ketchum cartoon, Dennis the Menace is saying his bedtime prayers. I can't pray, because I don't know what to say," laments Dennis to his mother.

"You don't have to worry about that," replies Mom. "There are no right words when talking to God. He understands everything."

"Really?" says Dennis. "Then I'll just say my ABC's, and God can put them together for me."

Sometimes, I can identify with Dennis. How about you? Words do not come easy in the presence of the Almighty. Life can be too puzzling, divine intimacy too threatening for words. In moments like these, we do well to remember that God knows how to hear us when we do not know how to pray. His spirit abides with our spirit, reminding us we are the children of God. Just give God the longings of your heart; let God do the rest.

Dear God, when words fail me in prayer, I know you are listening to my heart. I give thanks for your love. Amen.

Trapped

An infrequent traveler checked into a hotel room and immediately called the front desk for help. "I'm trapped inside my room," explained the traveler.

"How could you be trapped?" asked the clerk.

"Well, I see three doors," said the man. "The first opens into a closet; the second into a bathroom. And the third has a 'do not disturb' sign hanging on it."

I'm constantly meeting people who feel trapped in some room of life without a single clue of an exit. A marriage, a job, a life situation can leave us feeling isolated. There are openings and opportunities, but we can't for the life of us find them. Life with no exit is hell.

Maybe that's why Christ called himself a door. People who step into his presence go in and out, discovering life in all its fullness.

Dear God, help us never to lose hope but to trust in you always. Amen.

I.R.S.

As Ziggy in a Tom Wilson cartoon, leaves the I.R.S. office, the auditor says, "Remember, we will always be here for you."

You know, the promise of "always" sounds inviting, even from the Internal Revenue Service.

After all, what is always? Lovers promise to be present always. But divorces rob nearly all of that security. Friends hope to be friends forever, but time and tide tear people apart. Is anything for certain in this world other than death and taxes?

God is! Times change, people move, friends depart, children leave, families split. But God is the same yesterday, today, and forever. God will never leave us nor forsake us. God is with us always. Nearer than the I.R.S., greater than the threat of death, God is present—not for just an hour, not for just a day, not for just a year, but always.

Eternal God, we thank you that no matter how the darkness seems to surround us, you are always there to lead us into the light.
Amen.

Is Your God Too Small?

Is your God too small? Author J.B. Phillips posed that question in a book more than fifty years ago. Phillips says a lot of people cannot go deep into their own spiritual lives because their notions of God are too small. As long as God is confused with Santa Claus or a giant policeman, or a grandfather with a beard, we are not likely to get to know him very well. Somebody said, "God created us in his image and we have been returning the favor ever since. We have boxed God into our way of thinking."

All the while, God is omnipotent, omniscient, and omnipresent. He sets his footprint on the earth and rides upon the storm. When we let God out of the box, mighty and miraculous things begin to happen. Potential and possibilities appear. And we find ourselves saying, "Why didn't I think of that before?" Isn't it about time you let God be God?

God of creation, God of all, God of power and healing, how reassuring to know you are with us. Grant us that we never forget your goodness and power. Amen.

Picture of God

A little girl was deeply engaged with coloring crayons and paper at the kitchen table when her father asked her what she was doing. "I'm drawing a picture of God," replied the girl.

"How can you draw a picture of God?" inquired the dad. "Nobody knows what God looks like."

"They will when I finish my picture," said the little girl.

There are certainly parts of the Infinite that I don't understand. There are dimensions of Omnipotent that my small mind cannot comprehend. What is time to God who is from everlasting to everlasting? And exactly how does He have the whole world in His hands? The mysteries of God are beyond our explanation. Nevertheless, I am grateful to people, often children, who help me get a glimpse of the Almighty as He passes by. Their pictures of the Divine have given me faith to live by and hope to live on. They really do convince me that the essence of God is love. So if you really want to know God, look deeply into the eyes of a child.

Thank you, God, for the love of children, and for your love that transcends our understanding. Amen.

Better Than I Deserve

Better than I deserve: those four words summarize my life. When I consider the opportunities for ministry that have been mine at the places I have served I simply exclaim, "Better than I deserve." When I think about the friendships I have formed through the years that sustain me in the present, I simply exclaim, "Better than I deserve." When I think about the forgiving spirit people extend to me when I slip and fall, and the willingness of people to offer me another chance when I drop the ball, I know that it is better than I deserve.

In a *Family Circus* cartoon, Dolly turns to her mother on the front row of church as the congregation sings *Amazing Grace* and asks, exactly what did Grace do that made her so amazing? Grace gives us better than we deserve. Grace offers another chance. The grace that's brought us safe this far is able to lead us home. So the next time you count your blessings, consider your state in life, ponder your reason for being, see if you cannot agree with me. It's all been better than we deserve.

Lord, help us to remember that grace begins at the cross of Jesus. Only then can we accept love and live better than we deserve. Amen.

Churches

When it comes to Church, none is perfect, no not one. The Church may be the body of Christ for the world but churches are filled with fallible people. As long as God depends on people to do his work today, we will have to settle for something less than perfection.

Churches, however, do make a positive difference in society. The facts are in. Church goers contribute three times as much of their income to charitable causes as non-church goers. Church goers are twice as likely to volunteer for community service as non-church goers. Religiously involved teens, compared to unchurched youth, are much less likely to commit delinquent acts. Suppose you broke down in a crime ridden area of town and some strapping teenage boys approached you. Wouldn't you feel better to know they had just come from a Bible study instead of a drug party?

No, churches are far from perfect. Churches, however, continue to be God's best hope for humanity, and our best chance for community.

Thank you, loving God for your church.
We need a sanctuary to worship, pray and offer praise.
It's a place for sinners. Thanks be to God. Amen.

Make Overs

Extensive makeovers are big business these days. In 2002, there were 6.6 million of them done in the United States at an average cost of twenty thousand dollars each. Nearly a third of these were multiple procedures at the same time. We are a culture obsessed with looking better than we normally do.

What might be better than a new look is a new you? God is into more than cosmetic surgery. God offers to transform the whole person, not just do a tummy tuck. He can take our shriveled souls and our worn out lives and make them new again. He can restore in us a vibrancy of being; a joy to living that lasts forever. No life is too difficult; no problem is too large for God to transform.

So how about it, would you like to be a better person than you sometimes are? Could you use an injection of forgiveness or an infusion of unconditional love? The Great Physician would like to give your soul an extreme make over. Why not call him for a consultation today?

Dear God, help us understand the depth and height of your transforming love. Help us to accept and experience your love today and to love you in return. Amen.

Direction and Purpose

Meaning

In a *Peanuts* cartoon, Charlie Brown is lying in bed, pondering the big questions in life. "Sometimes I lie awake at night and I ask, 'Why am I here? What's the purpose of it all? Does life have any meaning?' Then a voice comes to me that says, 'Forget it! I hate questions like that!'"

Maybe we all hate questions like that, but from time to time we all lie awake at night asking them anyway. We were not put on earth to simply survive. We are here for a purpose, and we are made to ask the questions even when there are no easy answers. So, what are the questions that rumble through your mind in the middle of the night? Have you found a purpose for living? Is even a mundane day filled with meaning for you?

It can be. We can receive every sunrise as a special gift of God. We can live each moment with grace. We can fall asleep nightly knowing we have done what we could with what we have been given. Those are the things that sweet dreams are made of. Those are the answers to the riddles of life.

Merciful God, guide me to live a purpose-filled life by faithfully living as you would have me to do. Thanks be to God. Amen.

Direction

In Lewis Carroll's *Through a Looking Glass*, Alice wanders aimlessly through a strange kingdom until she comes to a fork in the road. She looks to the left, she looks to the right, and then exclaims, "Which way shall I go?"

That's when a Cheshire cat with a broad grin inquires, "Where are you going?"

Alice replies, "I don't know."

"Well," says the cat, "then it doesn't matter. If you don't know where you are going any road will get you there!"

Well how about it, do you know where you are going? Is your life shaped by purpose and determination to reach a desired destination? Anyone can wander, put in the time, take up space, and accomplish nothing. It takes purpose and planning along with motivation and willpower to get somewhere in life. So choose your roads wisely. Some lead to destruction. Others lead to everlasting life. The road you take can make all the difference.

On the road of life we have many choices to make.
Dear Heavenly Father, lead me to take the paths
leading to everlasting life. Amen.

Will of God

From time to time people come to me seeking the will of God for their lives. Over the years, I have discovered a thread to these quests that deserves to be tested a bit. People often assume God's will for their lives to be something difficult and painful. God can challenge us, but even those who have made great sacrifices for good causes seem not to have found wonderful joy in doing so.

So let me paint a different picture. What if God's will for you is something you enjoy? What if doing God's will is something delightful and meaningful? Does that strike you as something worth pursuing?

If joy is the true nature of God's will for me, then one way to find the will of God is to examine what I love to do. What are my passions? What gives me great delight? What do I feel good about when I am through? If we follow our hearts, we may find our true purpose for being, and in so doing, discover our real joy.

Lord Jesus, you have filled our hearts with joy, let us follow our hearts to determine your will for our lives. Amen.

Ship

A newly commissioned Navy captain took great pride in his first assignment as commander of a battleship. One stormy night, the captain saw a light moving steadily in their direction. He ordered the signalman to send this message: "Change your course ten degrees to the south!"

Quick came the reply: "change your course ten degrees to the north."

The new captain was not about to give in to another vessel, so he sent a counter message: "Alter your direction 10 degrees; I am the captain."

The answer flashed back promptly: "alter your direction; I am the lighthouse."

All of us would like to be masters of our fate and captains of our souls. Indeed we try to be. Even on collision courses we like to give orders and be in charge.

Yet, if we are truly wise, we learn to yield to higher powers and follow absolute directives. Such willingness to alter our courses will save us many collisions.

Loving God, it is so hard for us to "let go" and follow your directions. Give us the power to follow you and to let go. Thank You Dear Lord. Amen.

Einstein

Albert Einstein, so the story goes, was on a train trip to an out-of-town engagement. The conductor stopped by to punch Dr. Einstein's ticket. The great scientist, preoccupied with his work, rummaged through his coat pockets and brief case and with great embarrassment had to admit that he could not find his ticket. "We all know who you are," said the conductor, "Don't worry about it. Everything is okay."

"I know who I am too," replied Einstein. "What I don't know is where I am going."

In the rush and pressure of your life, do you know where you are going? When you reach your destination, will you know enough to stop? If we do not know where we are going, how can we hope to know when we arrive? So chart your future well. Good planning is essential to good living. And never get too busy to remember your destination. It's the only way to go.

Father God, in the rush and pace of our daily lives, we often fail to slow down enough to truly know where we are headed in life. Help us, Oh Lord, to feel Your presence so that we can find our way. Amen.

Vertigo

Flying over large bodies of water, airplane pilots encounter a danger called "vertigo." It's a condition where one becomes confused as to what is up, down, left, or right. Safety lies in following instruments instead of inclinations, facts instead of feelings.

Disorientation is a dangerous life condition, too. When suspended in space over some deep sea of life, it's tough to discern reality. Grief leaves us depressed. Divorce leaves us confused. Losses leave us wondering which way to turn. Stress raises our blood pressure but not our sense of direction.

In times like these, we need wisdom from above and help from others. We need instruments that keep the soul steadfast and sure while the billows roll. We need to be grounded in the word of God, connected to a community of faith, guided by good reason until the storm passes over and perspective returns to us again. Do you have the necessary equipment to fly through the storm?

Wonderful God, we need You to love us and guide us through life's storms. We need You to be the compass so that we can find our way. Amen.

Vision into Reality

Many years ago, Walt Disney took a group of people out to a piece of land in central Florida that had no use at all. It was marshy and muddy. The city of Orlando had written it off as useless. But, as Disney led this group of people through this rough acreage, he described in vivid detail the various structures, themes, rides, and excitement the park would bring. Walt Disney died during the construction of that theme park. At the grand opening of Disney World somebody said, "Isn't it too bad that Walt Disney didn't get to see this."

That's when Mike Vance, the creative director of Disney Studios, replied, "He did see it; that's why it is here."

Happy are those who have the eyes to see what can be and the determination to turn their vision into reality. They are the people who dream impossible dreams and fight unbeatable foes with a constant eye on the future. They are more than wishful thinkers. They are creative doers. They paint the pictures that future reality is made of.

We give thanks, dear Lord, for those who have great vision and determination; but for most of us we live each day unto itself. Thank you for caring for us as well. Amen.

Last Words

Two brothers terrorized a small town for decades. They were unfaithful to their wives, abusive to their children, and dishonest in business. They were loud, boisterous, and just plain rude to everyone. One day the younger brother died. That's when the older brother bribed a local pastor into conducting the funeral and into promising to include in the service a statement that his brother was a saint. On the day of the funeral, the pastor said, "Everyone here knows that the deceased was a wicked man, a womanizer, and a drunk. He terrorized employees and cheated on his taxes. But as evil and sinful as this man was, compared to his older brother, he was a saint."

When the day comes, as it surely will, that someone stands up to summarize your time on earth, will it take a bribe from family for something positive to be said or will the words of praise flow freely? A good life is not a sudden blaze of glory won. A good life is the accumulation of days in which good deeds are done.

Dear Jesus, help me to live each day of my life as best I can, so that when my days are done, my life will have had meaning and purpose. Amen.

Chinese Proverb

A Chinese proverb says, "If you wish to be happy for one hour, get drunk. If you desire to be happy for three days, get married. If you want to be happy for eight days, kill your pig and eat it. If you wish to be happy for a lifetime, learn to fish." Realizing that fishing is vocation not recreation for the Chinese, I began to wonder if I find happiness in the routine of the day? As the stream flows and the grass grows, as the demands of the day have their way, do I find happiness and joy?

The pursuit of happiness is an inalienable American right. Thomas Jefferson penned it into our Declaration of Independence. Americans have been running after it ever since. What is happiness? Must we have someone else to make us so very happy? Is happiness a matter of luck or a fortunate set of circumstances?

I believe happiness is an inside job to be found in the most routine of days. It is knowing who you are and what on earth you are supposed to do for heaven's sake.

Merciful Savior, we go about life seeking happiness when all we have to do is accept your love and grace for heaven's sake. Amen.

Get Up and Go

In a Jim Davis cartoon, Garfield the cat is lying in his box trying to coax himself into getting up. "It's time to spring into action!" says Garfield to himself.

"Huuuuut", says Garfield as he pounds his paw on the floor. Finally, in surrender, Garfield flops back down in the box with this lament. "The Spirit is willing, but the Springer is weak!"

Does that describe you this morning? Some days, it's just hard to get up and get going. We know we need to, we realize we have to, but we still just don't want to. Our "springer-upper" is weak.

If your get up and go, got up and went with the passing of time, maybe you need a new reason for being, a better purpose for going, a higher call to action. It's one thing to make a living. It's quite another thing to make a life. There are good reasons to get up and go to work, to stay put and raise your kids, to hang in there when the going is tough. It's called making a life for the people you love and giving back to the community you've got. It's putting in more than you take out. So get up and go for it.

Good Shepherd, lead us on the path of life to find purpose for each day. Help us to provide for our loved ones and give back to our community. Give us the energy to "get up and go." Amen.

Nowhere Fast

In a Tom Wilson Cartoon, Ziggy is standing in front of a huge road sign pointing the way to "Nowhere Fast."

How about it, are you speeding down the road to nowhere? On the highway of life, it's not the distance we cover as much as the direction we take that determines our destination. Sometimes we take a lot of time, burn a lot of energy, and leave a lot of pollution, traveling the fast lane to nowhere.

Several years ago, on a family vacation, my son leaned over the back seat of the station wagon and said, "Dad, when we get to where we are going, where will we be?"

Maybe that's the right question for you and me. It's not the "going" but the "getting there" that makes the difference. On this road trip called life, make sure the compass is pointing in the right direction.

Sometimes we feel like we are going nowhere fast. At these times, Lord, lift me up and show me the right direction. I know that I can't make it alone. Thank You Precious Lord. Amen.

Gone to the Dogs

The problem with people is that we too often act like dogs. Have you thought about that? On an evening walk through the neighborhood, a dog wants to stop at every smell and scratch at every flea. Dogs are easily distracted and readily annoyed. They are controlled by their environment and determined to follow their every whiff. A simple walk with a stubborn dog can be a tug of war.

Sometimes I wonder if we get so busy scratching where everybody itches and chasing our personal agendas that we become distracted from the true purposes of life and community. We cannot always have our own way and have community at the same tune. While my needs may be important, fixation on my needs can lead to a myopic view of life that fails to consider the well being of everyone. This is no time to let our community go to the dogs. Let us rise to the highest level of human potential and with the help of God, pursue liberty and justice for all.

Lord, You've called us to a higher purpose than just ourselves. Give us clear vision to see the needs of others, and the compassion to put the needs of others ahead of our own. Amen.

Busy

Have you ever stepped on an anthill? Ants come out of nowhere. They go crazy. They look like a city during rush hour, or a crowd leaving a football game.

Much like ants, we are busy people. We hurry here and run there. We go till we drop and never stop. Above all, we are keeping busy. Where did we get the idea that "busyness" was a virtue?

Sure, it's good to get things done. "Work" is a fine four-letter word. Involvement can instill interest. But, it's accomplishment, not busyness that makes all the difference.

Where is your vital balance? Are you too busy to take care of yourself; too busy to be with your family; too busy to talk with God? If so, your "busyness" may be robbing you of life, squeezing the juice of joy right out of your days.

Maybe it's time to restore the rhythm. As a wise prophet said long ago, "In returning the resting we shall be saved. In quietness and trust we shall find strength."

God Our Father, I treat time as if it's mine to control. Give me discernment to accomplish what you want me to accomplish, even when that disagrees with my priorities. Amen.

Don't Blow It

One day, when General Omar Bradley was traveling by commercial airline in an ordinary business suit, a young private sat down beside him on the plane. The gregarious young private, not recognizing the general, wanted to talk. "Let's get acquainted," said the young soldier, "You must be a banker."

The general, not wanting to be bothered by the private, responded, "I am General Omar Bradley, a five-star general in the United States Army. I am head of the Joint Chiefs of Staff at the Pentagon in Washington, D. C."

The stunned kid thought for a moment and then replied, "Well sir, that's a very important job; I sure hope you don't blow it."

Whether or not we are generals or heads of staffs, most of us have very important jobs. It would be of benefit to many that we do not blow it. There are people counting on us day by day to do our jobs well. Why not be the best you can be for the glory of God and the good of people?

*Lord, you have fashioned me in your image,
so why do I "blow it" so often? Please strengthen me
every moment of the day so that those whose lives I touch
can truly count on me to do my job well,
whatever it may be. Amen.*

Sports

Race

Every year the world watches the Kentucky Derby. However, as the world turns attention to Louisville's big horse race, let us not forget the human race. On the tracks of life there are no spectators, only participants. The purpose of the human race is not to separate the winners from the losers, but to make the finish line together. Mud slinging must be minimized in the human race, the urge to get ahead forsaken. The rules of a horse race and the rules of the human race are dramatically different. Sometimes I wonder if we comprehend that?

As you connect with the human race during this horse race, practice random acts of kindness. Respect is a fundamental rule. Dignity is needed through and through. Before you criticize or abuse, walk a mile in the other person's shoes. Let the up and out join hands with the down and out that all may complete the race that is set before them. So when life is done and the sun is setting and it's all too soon a race that's run, may we be found then, together in the winner's circle, hearing the Owner of all saying, "Well done."

Maker of heaven and Earth, help us to remember who we are, to practice kindness, and to show respect towards others. Amen.

Game of Life

Loving God, you have created us in your image and claimed us as your own. Before we belonged to anyone else, we belonged to you. You knitted us together in our mother's womb and carved our names on the palms of your hands. Even the hairs on our head are numbered by you. So dear Lord, you have searched us and known us. You know our coming in and going out, and even now we find ourselves recipients of your love and care.

We praise you for the privilege of playing together on the fields of life. May this game be played with joy and excitement, with purpose and determination, with integrity and sportsmanship. Be present at this game, O Lord. Let us treat others as we would like to be treated ourselves. May all our actions be pleasing in your sight. In victory or defeat, may we bring you honor and glory.

Bless those who bring to this game unusual fears and difficulties. Help us know that no trouble enjoys eternal life. Make us aware that your grace is sufficient for every need.

Most of all gracious God, make us all winners in the big game of life. Teach us the joy of teamwork and the courage to believe that you will never leave us nor forsake us.

Loving God, we pray that we may be participants and not just spectators in the game of life. Amen.

Success or Significance

Arizona Cardinals safety Pat Tillman walked away from a 3.6 million dollar NFL contract to join the Army after the attacks of September 11. He was killed by friendly fire while serving in Afghanistan. At Pat's memorial service, Senator John McCain said, "While many of us will be blessed to live a longer life, few of us will live a better life."

Success or significance? Which will it be for you? Some people know no reason to be born, save to consume the corn, eat the fish, and leave behind a dirty dish. Others trade success for significance. They want their lives to matter and they commit themselves to making a difference wherever they can. They ask not what their country can do for them; they ask what they can do for their country.

It's been said that people all wrapped up in themselves make mighty small packages. So why not break out of your self-centeredness and discover the joy of serving? There is good you can do, help you can render, a difference you can make today and every day. Isn't it about time to get started?

Oh Lord, may our lives have significance.
Teach us to use our abilities so that we may make a difference.
Amen.

Encouragement

Football Coach Bear Bryant was a legend in his own time. He never suffered many losses on the football field. When faced with the possibility, the coach was able to say or do something that would turn the tide. One time, when his team went into the locker room at half time, three touchdowns behind, Bear Bryant searched for the right words to motivate his players. He took one look at his downtrodden team and in a booming voice said, "Now we've got these fellows just where we want them." With that, his team went back on the field and won the game.

Most of us could use some encouragement like that. We don't need to know what we've done wrong as much as we need to know there is still within us, in the time left to us, the power to overcome. Some of our greatest strengths are discovered when we are down, but not yet out. From the ashes of discouragement come the fires of victory when fanned by the right person at the right time in the right way.

Help us Lord to give words of encouragement to those who are discouraged so that they find strength to endure and to overcome hardships through your love for them. Amen.

Baseball

In 1986 Bob Brenley was playing 3rd base for the San Francisco Giants. In the 4th inning of a game with the Atlanta Braves, Brenley made an error on a routine grounder. Four batters later, he kicked away another grounder, then threw wildly to home plate committing two more errors. A few minutes later, Bob muffed another play to become the only major league player to make four errors in one inning.

Bob Brenley could have given up, but he didn't. In the bottom of the 5th, he hit a home run. In the bottom of the 7th he hit a single, driving in two runs to tie the game. In the bottom of the 9th, Bob Brenley hit a massive home run into the left field seats to win the game for the Giants.

Whether you are playing baseball, or trying to make a hit in life, never let your errors get you down. Step to the plate with confidence and become a winner.

*Dear Lord, teach us never to give up.
Help us to be determined to succeed in whatever we do. Amen.*

Objective Case

As Garrison Keillor tells it, the town ball club was called the Lake Wobegon Schroeders, so named because the starting nine were all brothers, sons of E.J. Schroeder.

E.J. was always ticked off. If a boy hit a bad pitch, E.J. would spit, curse, and rail at him. If a son hit a home run, E.J. would say, "Your grandma could have put the wood on that one since the wind practically took it out of here."

No one could please him. One day against Freeport, a long ball was hit toward the center field fence. E.J. Jr. went for it, and when he could not reach it, Junior threw his glove forty feet in the air, managed to snag the ball, and then caught both ball and glove as they came down. The crowd roared. Even old E.J. himself clapped his hands. But by the time Jr. got back to the dugout, the old man said, "I saw that catch once before in Superior, Wisconsin, only it was night and the ball was a lot harder to catch."

It's been said that some people are just born in the objective case. Do kind words stick in your throat or flow from your lips? An encouraging word can make a world of difference.

Many times we find fault in others and fail to see the good. At those times, gracious God, help us to stop and find words of encouragement, not criticism. Amen.

Batting 500

A troubled man paid a visit to his rabbi. "Rabbi" said he, wringing his hands. "I'm a failure. More than half the time I do not succeed in doing what I must do. Will you help me?"

"Ah my son", replied the Rabbi. "Try this wisdom. Go and look on page 930 of the *New York Times Almanac* for the year 1970, and you will find peace of mind."

The man did. On that page of the *New York Times Almanac*, the man found a listing of the lifetime batting averages of history's best baseball players. Ty Cobb, the greatest slugger of them all, had a lifetime average of .367.

So the man went back to the Rabbi and said, "Ty Cobb: .367. Is that the answer?"

"Sure is," replied the rabbi. "If the greatest batter in baseball history got a hit about once in every three times at bat, why are you feeling a failure about batting .500?"

A perspective like that ought to encourage us all to step up to the plate of life one more time.

Wonderful God, help us to keep trying and not be discouraged when we fail. We know life eternal is waiting. Thanks be to God. Amen.

Pistol Pete

Pistol Pete Maravich was one of basketball's most dazzling players. At LSU, he set many records that still stand today. In his autobiography *Heir To a Dream*, he writes how he considered basketball the ultimate supplier of all his needs. But in spite of records, fame, and wealth, Pistol Pete lacked joy and meaning. He finally found his true purpose in life through a personal relationship with Jesus Christ.

What is your reason for being? Are you trying to find ultimate meaning through work, family, sports, or hobbies? Beware! It's just not there. While success is a worthy victory, life is a moving target. What seems so important today pales in value tomorrow. Even our children grow up and develop a mind of their own.

So why not let the one who created you also fulfill you? We were made for a relationship with our maker, and we will be forever restless until we find our rest in him. So why not make a real New Year's resolution? Connect with God this year.

God of love, fill us with joy and meaning; bring us closer to you so that we can have a relationship with Jesus Christ. Amen.

Inspiration

It was the spring of 1995 and professional golfer Ben Crenshaw was in Augusta, Georgia, preparing for the Masters. "Nothing could be better," thought Crenshaw, "than to win the Masters again." Then the phone call came. Ben's long time friend and teacher Harvey Penick had died.

Ben flew to Austin for the funeral, then flew back to Augusta determined to play his best golf ever. As he burst into tears at the 18th green, they were not just the tears of joy over winning. They were tears of gratitude for his beloved teacher.

All of us have somebody to whom we owe a great debt of gratitude for teaching us the game of life. At the top of the board is none other than God. Have you stopped to say thanks lately?

We give thanks to you, Dear Lord, for our many blessings and for those who have made a difference in our lives. Amen.

Education

Mohammad Ali built a reputation, not only from his punches in the boxing ring, but his punch lines in the rounds of life. Ali, talking with a young man about to drop out of college, offered this precise advice:

> "Stay in college, get the knowledge,
> And stay there till you're through.
> If they can make penicillin out of moldy bread,
> They can surely make something out of you."

Well, whatever way you put it, education is essential to our individual and community development. Enlightenment is a lifeline to the future. It provides a window of opportunity and a doorway of hope for every generation. I will be eternally grateful for the teachers and pastors of my past who, through a pat on the shoulder and sometimes a kick in the pants, kept me plowing new ground of educational opportunity. They had the ability to see gold worth mining in this soul of mine, and that made all the difference.

Dear Lord, thank you for teachers and those people in our lives who have encouraged us and supported us in gaining an education. Amen.

Storms of Life

Questions

Life is full of questions. Have you noticed that? Take a stroll with any child and you will be bombarded with questions. Why is the sky blue? Why do flowers bloom? How do birds sing? If you stay in touch with that child long enough the questions deepen with age. Who is God? My friend down the street is dying with cancer, am I going to die? Even when we become adults, the questions linger. Why do bad things happen to good people? Why do the evil prosper? Life is full of questions.

I have discovered the key to life is not finding answers to all the questions. The key to life is living the questions. Oh, I know, we like answers. We want to get this problem solved so we can go on the next one and the next one until one day we get our questions answered and then we die. That is not living. Life is a riddle that has no easy answer.

The riddles of life are great teachers. The problems of life demand great faith. And I go on, not knowing.

Dear God, life is a mystery to be lived by faith.
Help me to grow in my faith journey and help me to accept
that I will never fully understand its meaning. Amen.

Hope and Faith

Theologian Reinhold Niebuhr once said, "Nothing worth doing is completed in our lifetime, so we are saved by hope. And nothing true or good makes complete sense in any immediate context of history; therefore we are saved by faith."

So, how about it? Are you living by hope and faith? Hope is like water to a fish or air to a jumbo jet. It is basic to life. And faith is the courage to believe where we cannot see and the willingness to wait for the unknown to be revealed. We cannot stay on the road to anticipated dreams without faith and hope- at least not very long.

So, it is a hopeful day in any person's life when we start making investments that we will not see to maturity in our lifetime. People of faith do not know all the answers. We do not have it all worked out. We just have the courage to keep walking in the dark until we come to the light. And that makes all the difference.

Dear Jesus, strengthen me in my faith and fill me with your love so that each day is filled with hope and courage. Amen.

Singing in the Rain

I was awakened on a rainy morning recently with the sound of birds singing. As I lay there enjoying my private concert, I marveled at the ability of birds to sing in all kinds of circumstances. Even in a storm a bird sits on a branch and makes music. Then it dawned on me; birds sing because they have wings. If the branch breaks, the bird flies. Birds are made to survive the storm.

There is a popular song that invites people to sing in the rain. If it happens to be a child-like frolic through a spring shower, then the invitation is enticing. But what if the storms are raging? Well, that's another matter, unless of course we have wings. It takes wings to sing in the storm. That's why immortality is more than whistling in the dark to avoid the ghost of death. It is the joyful song of triumph over life's most destructive forces. It is the glad assurance that if I take up the wings of the morning and fly to the uttermost parts of the sea, even there God will guide me. His strong hand will hold me tight.

Help me, God, to live with a song in my heart, and guide me through life's struggles knowing that you are holding me tight. Amen.

Hurricane

As we continue to help the people of various states recover from hurricanes and other disasters, I am reminded of a story that came from hurricane Andrew in 1992. The storm devastated thousands of houses in South Florida. But in one area, where the wreckage looked like a war zone, one house remained standing, fully anchored to its foundation. A reporter asked the owner why his house was not blown away.

The shy Floridian replied, "I built this house myself. I built it according to the Florida Hurricane Code. When it called for two by six trusses, I used two by six trusses. I built it to endure the storm and it did."

Into every life the rains come, the winds blow, and the floods rise. Morning never wears to evening without some heart breaking, a heart just as sensitive as yours and mine. Here's the question. Are you building a life that will endure the storm? When life beats you and defeats you, when life plays havoc with your ordered ways, are you made of the stuff that stands the test of time?

Dear Lord, give me the strength to endure the storms of life.
We give thanks and praise to you. Amen.

Detours

"Detour Ahead." Don't you hate to see that sign on your way to some desired destination? Detours mean delays, alternate routes, and often winding roads.

Life too is cluttered with detours. Our fixed dreams and our greatest hopes have a way of slamming into brick walls, forcing us to find a way through, over, under, or around in order to travel on. So, here are a few suggestions for the detours of your life:

Face the facts. When it says the divorce is final, the divorce is final. No fantasy will resurrect it in the night.

Compensate the best you can. When one part of the body is removed, other companion parts become stronger. The same is true for our souls.

Regain perspective. No detour lasts forever. No trouble enjoys everlasting life. This too shall pass. If we can't get over it, we can certainly get through it or find some other creative way to endure it.

Dear God, help us to find our way when we are faced with the detours of life. Our faith is in you, Christ Jesus. Amen.

Through It All

Andrae Crouch has recorded fifteen albums, received nine Grammy awards, and worked on musical scores for *The Lion King* and *The Color Purple*. He has been nominated for an academy award and performed for presidents and kings. That is not bad for a boy who had no formal musical training and still cannot sight-read music. Andrae had to overcome stuttering as a boy and still struggles with dyslexia. His mother, father, and brother all died within a span of two years. Still, he finds the courage to pastor an inner city church in California.

My favorite of Crouch's music is a piece called "Through It All." One stanza goes like this:

> "I thank God for the mountains, I thank him for the valleys. I thank him for the storms he's brought me through. For if I'd never had a problem, I wouldn't know that God could solve them. I wouldn't know what faith in God could do."

Have you learned to trust God through it all? God never said life would be easy. He only promised to give us courage for the challenge.

Thank you, O God, for your constant and unconditional love that provides us the strength to endure and overcome hardships. Give us strength for today. Amen.

Weight of the World

A giant statue of the Greek god Atlas stands at the entrance of the RCA building in New York City. The beautifully proportioned Atlas, with all his muscles straining, is holding the world on his shoulders. There he is, the most powerfully built man in the world, barely able to stand under his load.

Across the street is St. Patrick's Cathedral. Behind the high altar is a little shrine of the boy Jesus, eight or nine years old. He's holding the world in one hand, with no effort at all.

Sooner or later all of us feel the weight of the world falling in on us. Disease strikes. Death comes. Employment ends. Children wander. The list is endless. In moments like these, we make a decision. We can stretch every nerve and strain every muscle trying to carry the load ourselves. Maybe we will succeed, or we can surrender every situation, let go of every concern, and trust the One who's got the whole world in His hands to bear the weight for us. Of that, I am certain.

Help us, Lord, to place our burdens with you. May we grow in our faith. We give thanks and praise to your Holy Name. Amen.

Adversity

A young woman was complaining to her father about the difficulties of life. Instead of challenging her argument, the Dad decided to give his daughter a demonstration. "Meet me in the kitchen," said the father, "there's something I want to show you."

There, the dad set three pans of water to boiling. To the first pan he added carrots. Into the second, he dropped an egg. Then he took some ground coffee and scattered it into the third pan. After all three had cooked a while, he put their contents into separate bowls and asked his daughter to cut into the carrots and eggs while smelling the coffee.

The daughter, far from being amused, asked her father what he had in mind. "Well," said the delighted dad, "each food teaches us something about adversity. The hard carrot was softened by it. The fragile egg was hardened by it. And, the coffee changed the water into a tasty drink. Exactly what are you going to let adversity do to you?

Lord God, help us to face adversity and teach us how to deal with it. We cannot do it by ourselves, but pray for your guidance and love. Amen.

Mourning

Tuesdays with Morrie is a touching book about Morrie Schwartz, a Brandeis University professor who is dying of Lou Gehrig's disease, and his former student, Mitch Albom, who flies from Detroit to Boston every Tuesday to visit his beloved teacher. One day during their conversations, Mitch asks Morrie, "Do you ever feel sorry for yourself?"

Morrie thought a moment and then replied, "Sometimes in the mornings, that's when I mourn. I feel around my body and mourn what I have lost. I give myself a good cry, if I need it."

"But then I stop mourning. I concentrate on all the good things still in my life. I think about the people I will see through the day. I think about your visits on Tuesdays. I think about all the good stories I am going to hear. I don't allow myself any more self-pity than that. I get my mourning done in the mornings."

All of us have losses. All of us need to grieve. But let us beware lest grief and self-pity choke the life right out of us. There are good reasons for all of us to keep living.

Dear Lord, give me the strength of a Morrie Schwartz that I might deal with life's challenges and find purpose for each day. Keep me from feeling sorry for myself. Amen.

Inside Job

Abraham Lincoln once said that people are just about as happy as they make up their minds to be. Happiness has more to do with choice than circumstance. It is a matter of decision more than the fate of destiny. Have you found that to be true?

As for today, which will it be for you? Will you concentrate on disease, debt, doubt, disaster, discouragement, depression, danger, defeat, disagreement, and desolation? Or will you focus on thoughts of peace, plenty, power, persistence, patience, purpose, promotion, prayer, possibilities? The "D's" or the "P's:" which will it be for you today?

Happiness really is an inside job. I've seen too many miserable people who ought to have it made and too many happy people who are walking through some awful tragedy of life to believe otherwise. The soul is dyed the color of its thoughts. That's not fantasy. It's reality. So why not determine now to make this a good day whatever the circumstances may be?

God of Abraham, be with us that we can see the good in life. Help us to smile, sing a song, and find happiness in all circumstances. We give You praise. Amen.

What Happens To You

"It's not what happens to you but what you do with what happens to you that makes all the difference." For years, I have proclaimed that motto. Now I am trying to live by it.

Like thousands of others, I begin this new year (2005) fighting a new battle in an old war with cancer. Statistically, I am a cancer victim striving to become a cancer survivor. Personally, I consider myself a cancer warrior. I hate the stuff. This enemy, that has become a recurring thorn in my flesh, demands too much attention and controls too much of my life. I would rather be snow skiing than PET scanning. I prefer vacation hideaways to extended hospital stays. I've just not found anything exciting about the world of medicine, although I am deeply grateful to those who do.

Of course, cancer is not an elective course in the curriculum of life, but once enrolled, it's up to us to make the most of it. There are lessons to be learned, friends to be found, gratitude to be felt, and life to be lived at this university of hard knocks, and I intend to make the most of it. Thanks for all your prayers.

Lord Jesus, be with us in our battles with disease.
Help us to remain strong and to find solace in knowing that we are not in this alone and have you as our companion. Amen.

Boll Weevil

The people of Coffee County, Alabama, built a monument to misery. In the town square, a visitor can find a stone on which these words are inscribed, "In profound appreciation for the boll weevil, and what it has done as the herald of prosperity."

The tiny beetle destroyed Coffee County's cotton crops. The damage was devastating. Adversity, however, forced a change. Farmers began to plant peanuts. George Washington Carver had discovered hundreds of industrial uses for peanuts. Farmers, however, had been reluctant to change. The boll weevil eliminated the option and the results proved to be prosperous. Good grew out of perceived trouble.

When trouble threatens to undo you, recognize its danger, but don't despair. Crisis creates opportunity. Endurance designs character. Character produces hope.

Oh Lord, help us to recognize opportunity when times are bad. Out of bad, good can come. Help us to endure difficult times. We ask in Christ's name. Amen.

Usher

A young man applied for a job as an usher at a local movie theater. The manager interviewed the prospective employee. Finally, he got around to the what-to-do-in-an-emergency question? So the manager asked the kid, "And what would you do in case of a fire?"

"Oh, don't worry about me," replied the young man. "I'd be able to get out okay." What the potential employee failed to realize was that others were in the theater with him, and he had some responsibility for them.

Is that not a parable of life? No man is an island; no man walks alone. We do not cross the stage of life by ourselves. Others are with us. While they may be strangers, we cannot ignore them. For like the potential usher, we have a responsibility for their safety and security. Look all around you, find someone in need. Help somebody today. Though it be little, a neighborly deed. Help somebody today. There are persons stuck on the road of life, drowning in the demands of the day, dangerously close to the fires of some disaster. Should we not feel compelled to help them?

Lord, there are people within my reach every day that I can help. I pray for a discerning heart and a willing hand to do good in the world around me. Amen.

Flexibility

Flexible people seldom get bent out of shape. Have you considered that? Let me say it again. Flexible people seldom get bent out of shape. Life has a way of bending, stretching, and pulling us into positions that we never dreamed possible. Through such twists of time and turns of circumstances, we are left to wonder if we are going to break into pieces. Some people do. But it doesn't have to be that way. Flexible people learn to roll with the punches, adjust to the times, grow with the occasions, and glean from their experiences. Flexible people don't break; they bend. They don't let events determine their attitudes, their thoughts, and especially not their actions. They make adjustments when adjustments are necessary. They stay in shape instead of getting out of shape.

So, how about it? Are you prepared to be flexible today? When life comes at you with the unexpected and demands from you what you doubt to be in you—don't break; bend.

God, grant me the serenity to accept the things I cannot change, courage to change the things I can, and wisdom to know the difference. Amen.

Conflict

There's an old African proverb that says, "When the elephants fight, the grass suffers." Maybe we need to keep that in mind the next time we face a conflict. Conflict is a fact of life. People do have disagreements, get aggravated with one another, and even find themselves ready to fight. Before we let the conflict accelerate, we might do well to stop, step back, and consider the consequences of our actions.

When the elephants fight, the grass suffers. Children get hurt when parents quarrel. Communities decline when leaders continually disagree. Churches split when members can't get along. Screaming dissidents may make good talk show programs, but they seldom lead to better communication. So we must find a better way.

Let us learn to disagree without being disagreeable. Let us practice the art of conflict resolution. Let us work through our problems for the good of others, lest the green grass of understanding be reduced to the mud holes of hate and bitterness.

Lord, too often my tongue is used for hurt.
Help me rather to use my words for blessing others and stilling conflict.
Amen.

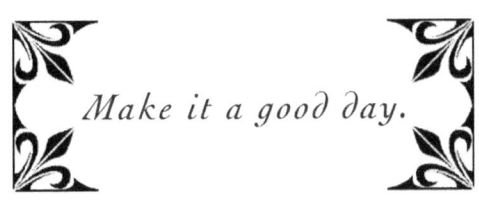

Make it a good day.